CHRISTMAS COLORING BOOK (DESIGN ORIGINALS) WITH EASY AND CUTE CHRISTMAS COLORING DESIGNS FOR GIRLS

Girls Coloring Book

ISBN: 9798571568845

Copyright 2020 © Crazy Craft

All Right Reserved.

Copyright 2020 © Crazy Craft

All Right Reserved.

All rights reserved. No part of this publication may be reproduced or used in any from or by any means- graphic, electronic, mechanical, including photocopying,recording, or information stroage and retrival without permission of the publisher.

The designs in this book are intended for the personal, noncommercial use of the retail purchaser and are under federal copyright laws; they are not to be reprodeced in any from for commercial use. Permission is granted to photocopy content for the personal use of the retail purchaser.

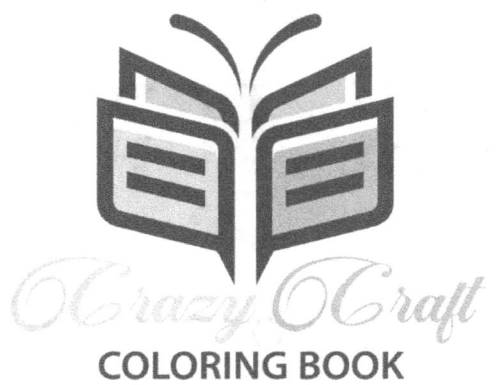

Have question ? Let us know.

crazycraftcoloringbook@gmail.com

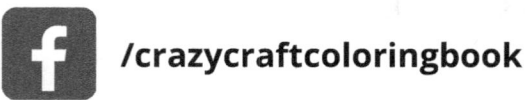 /crazycraftcoloringbook   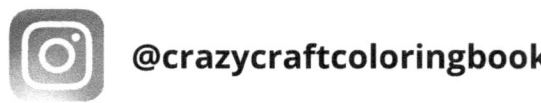 @crazycraftcoloringbook

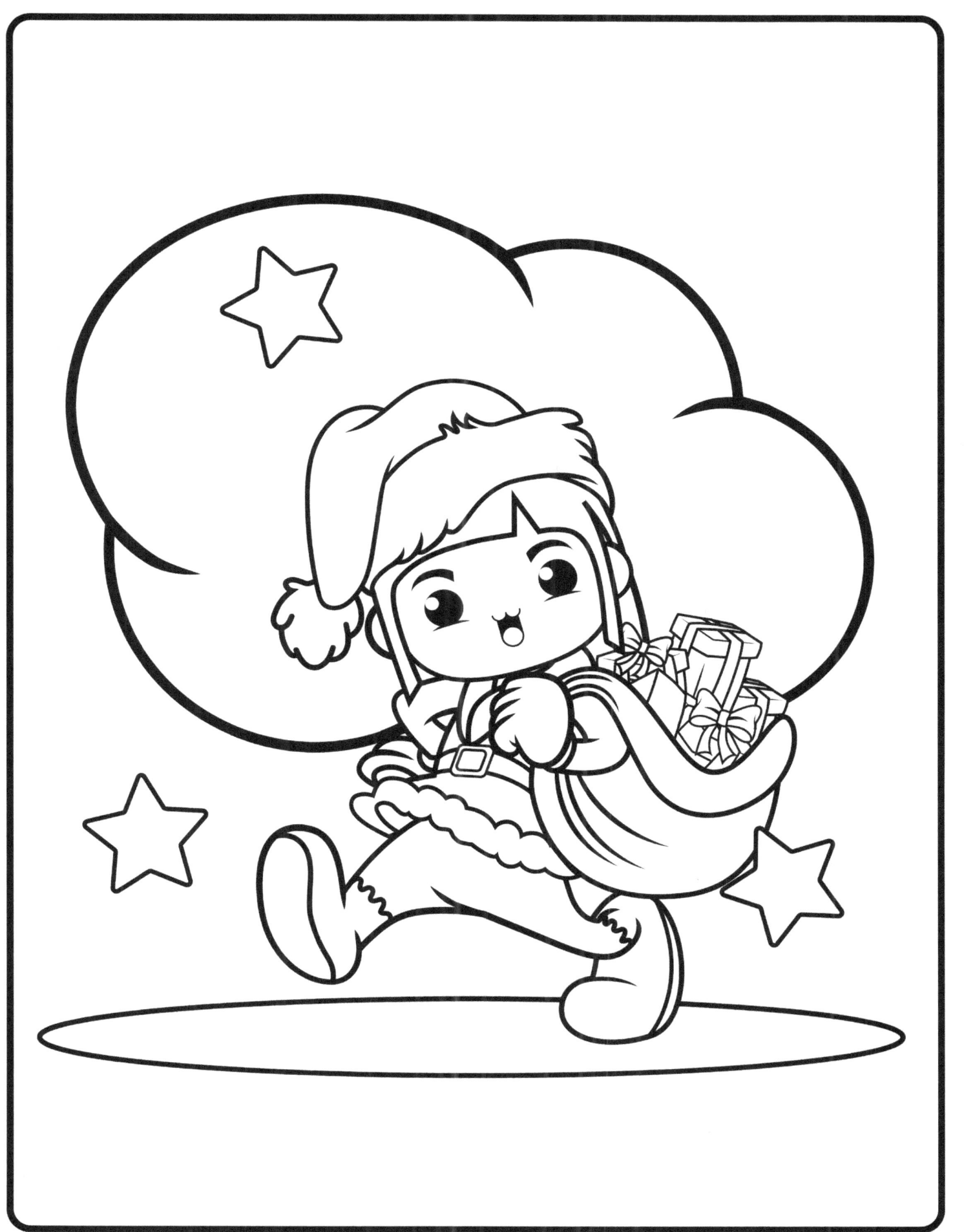

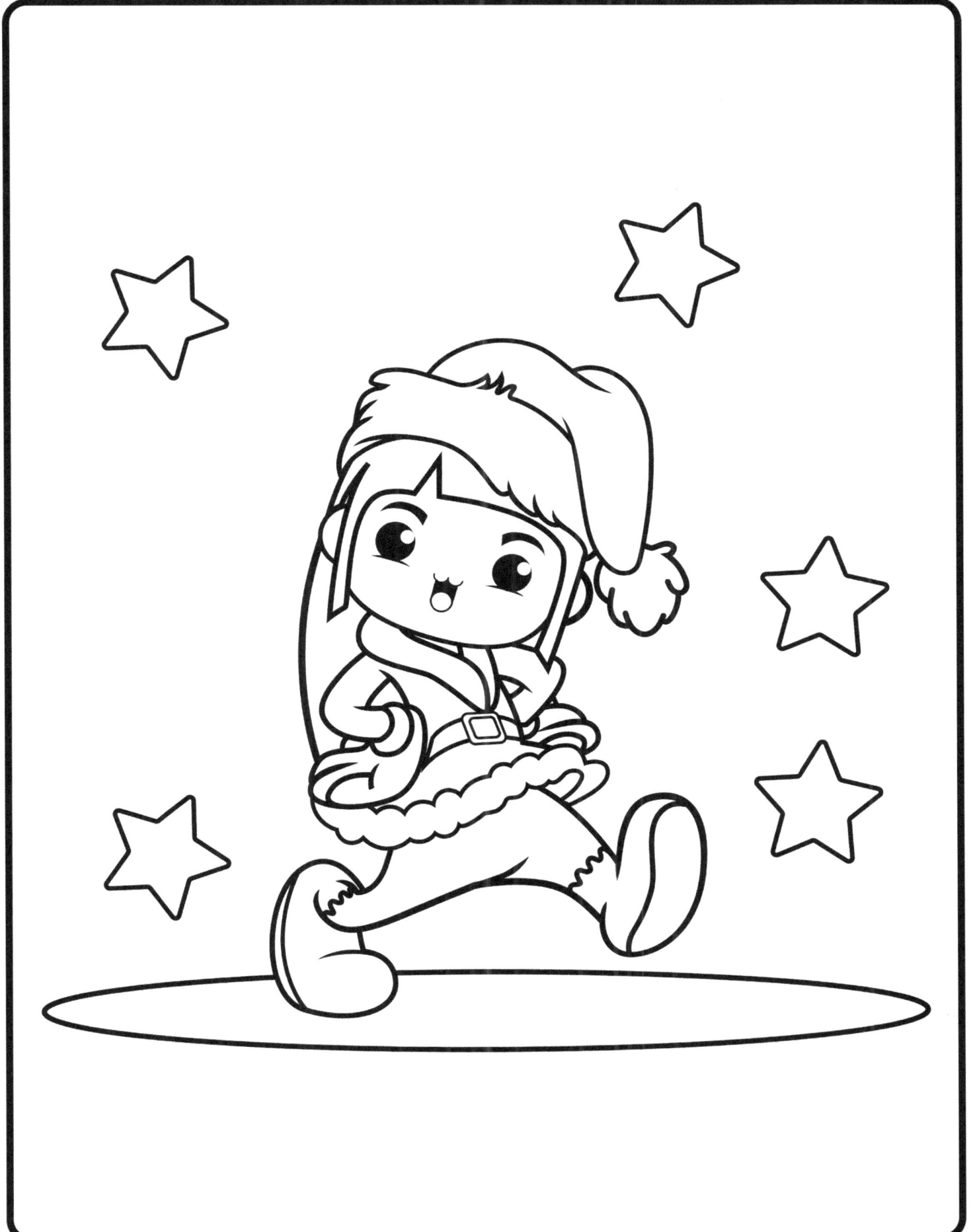

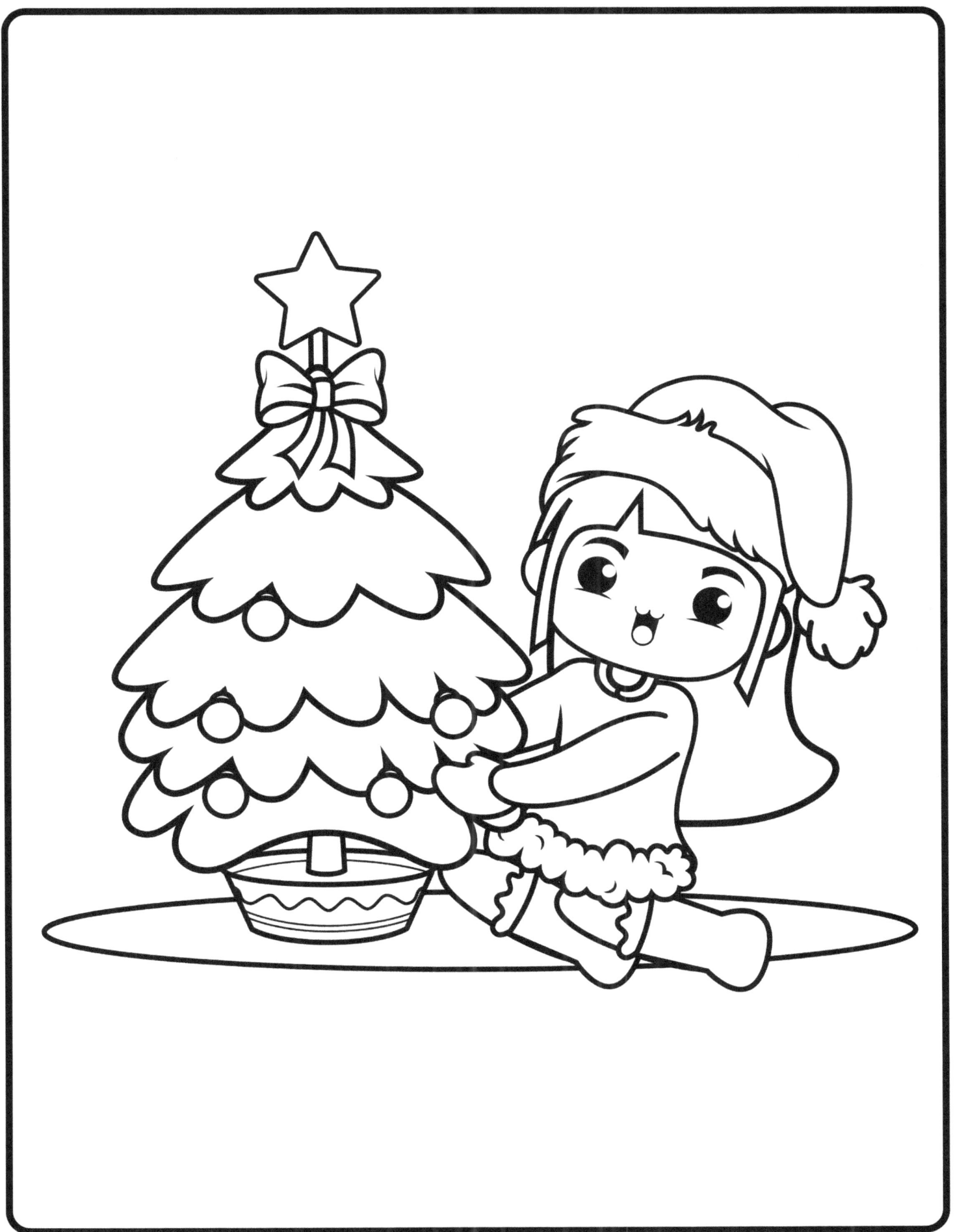

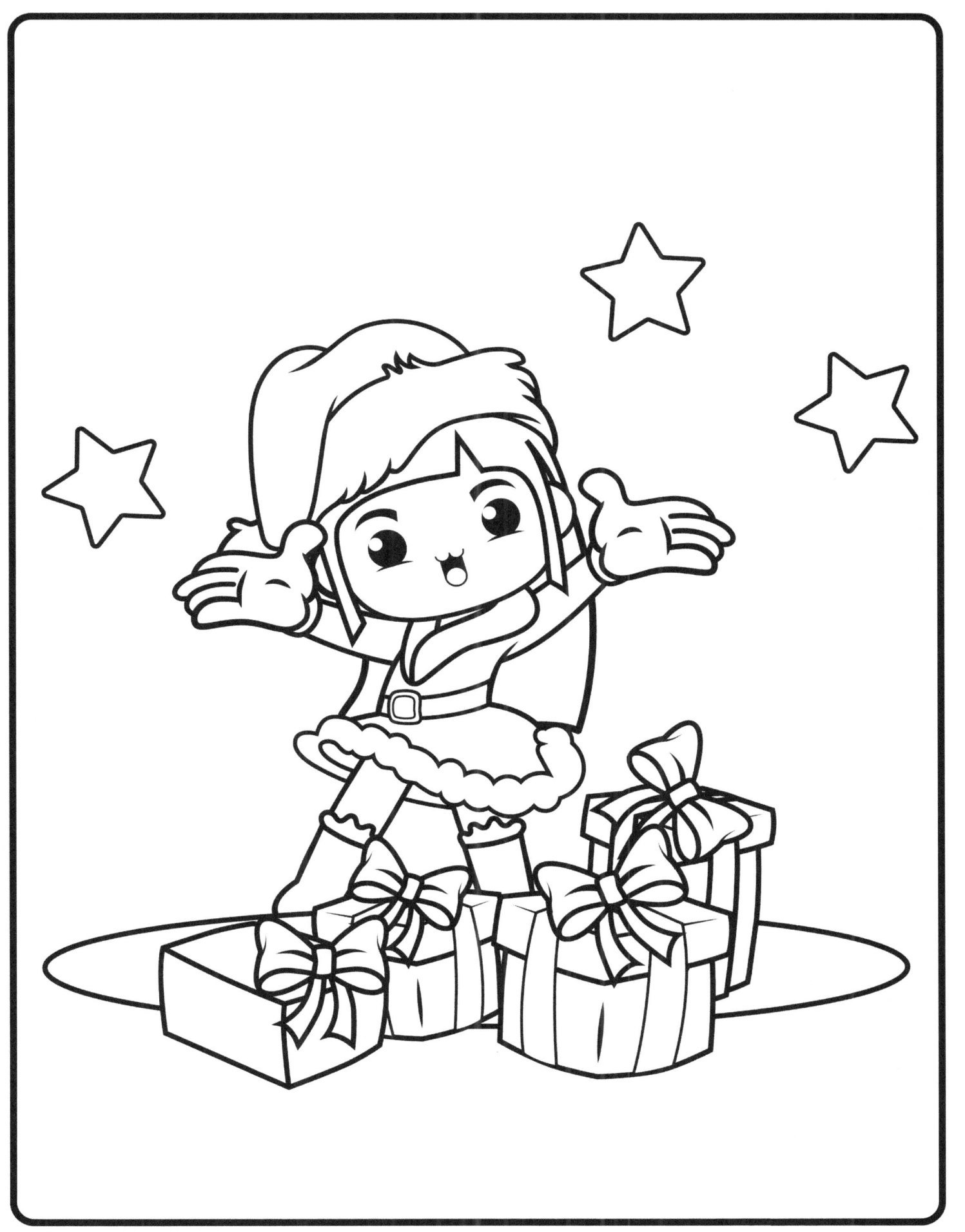

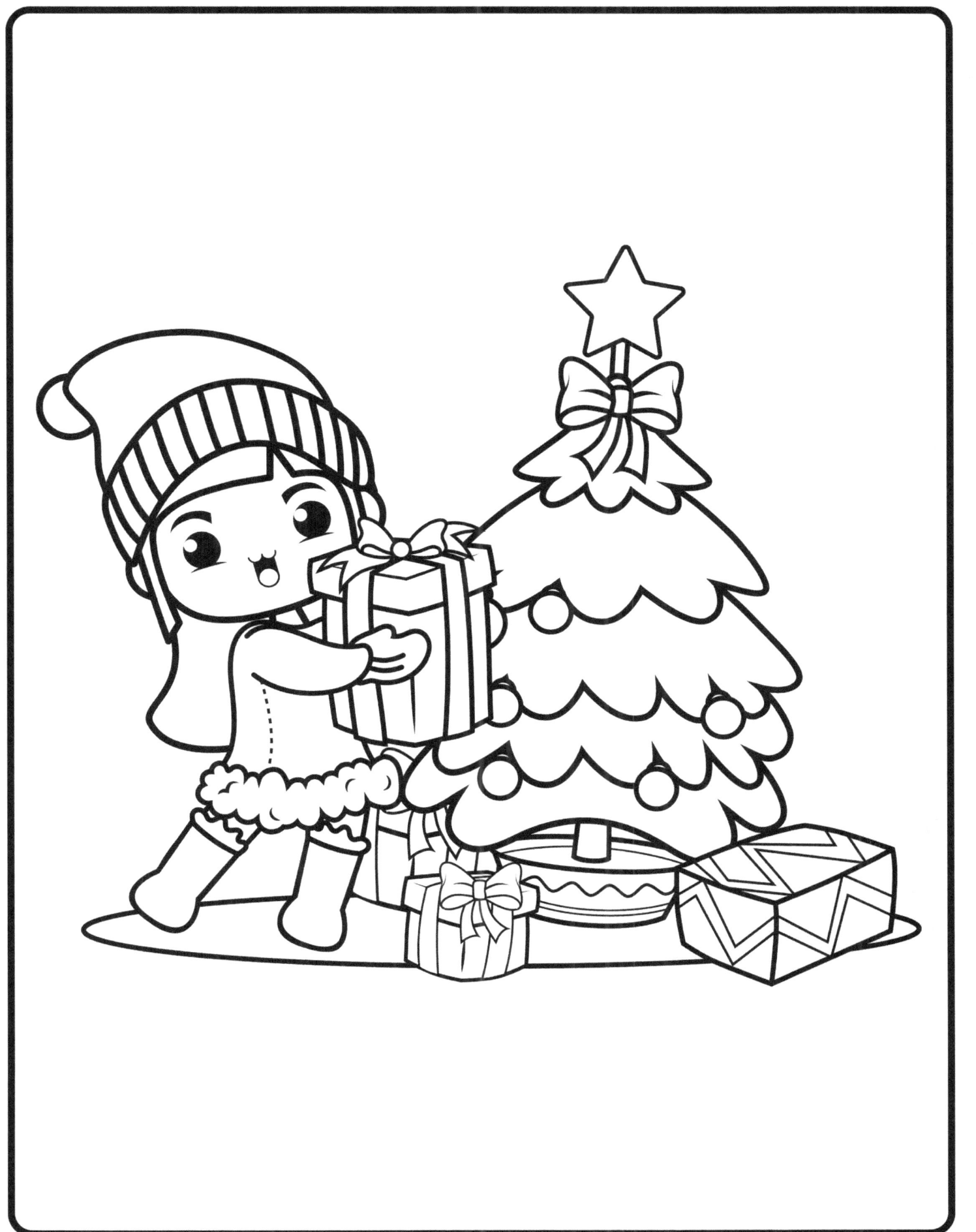

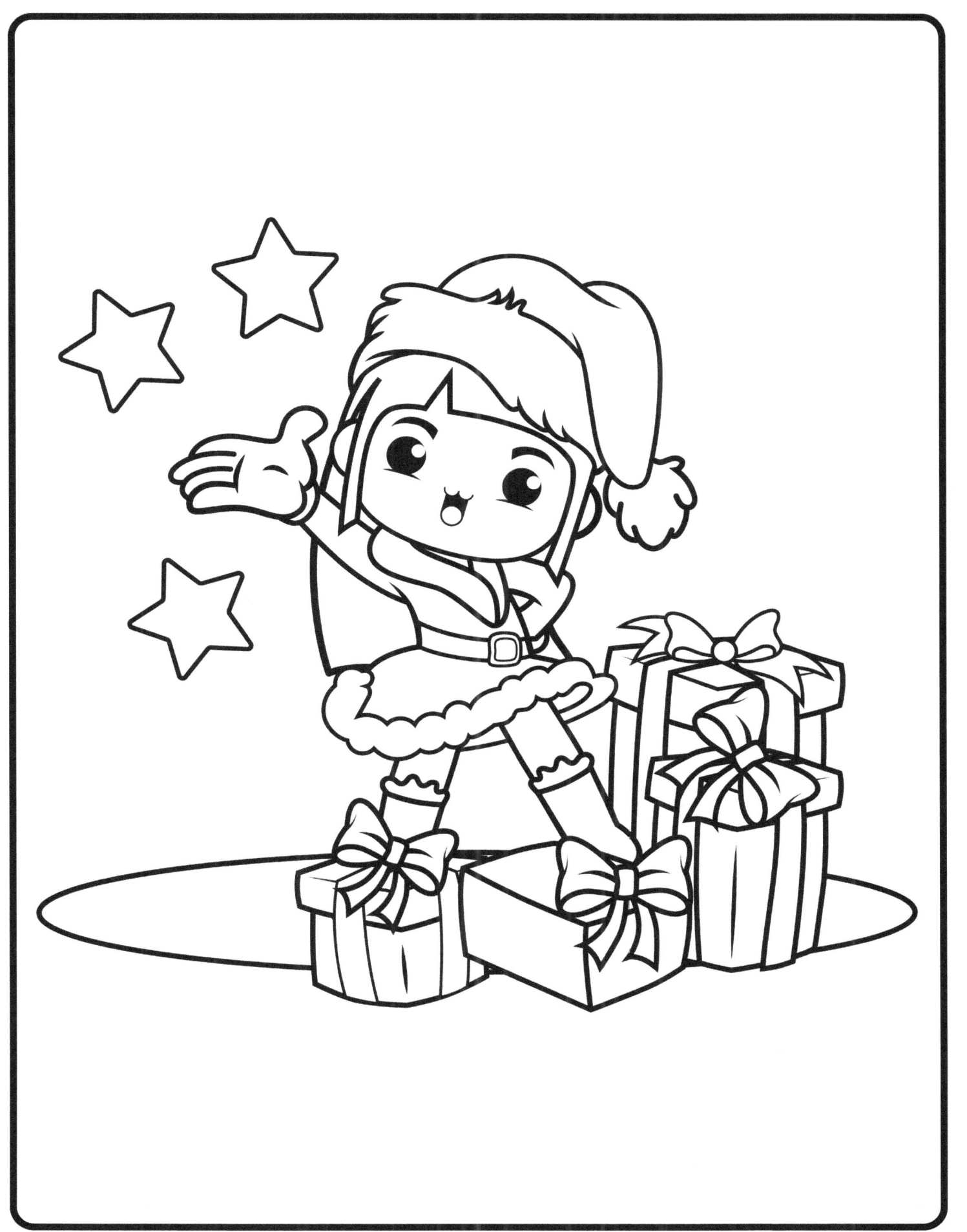

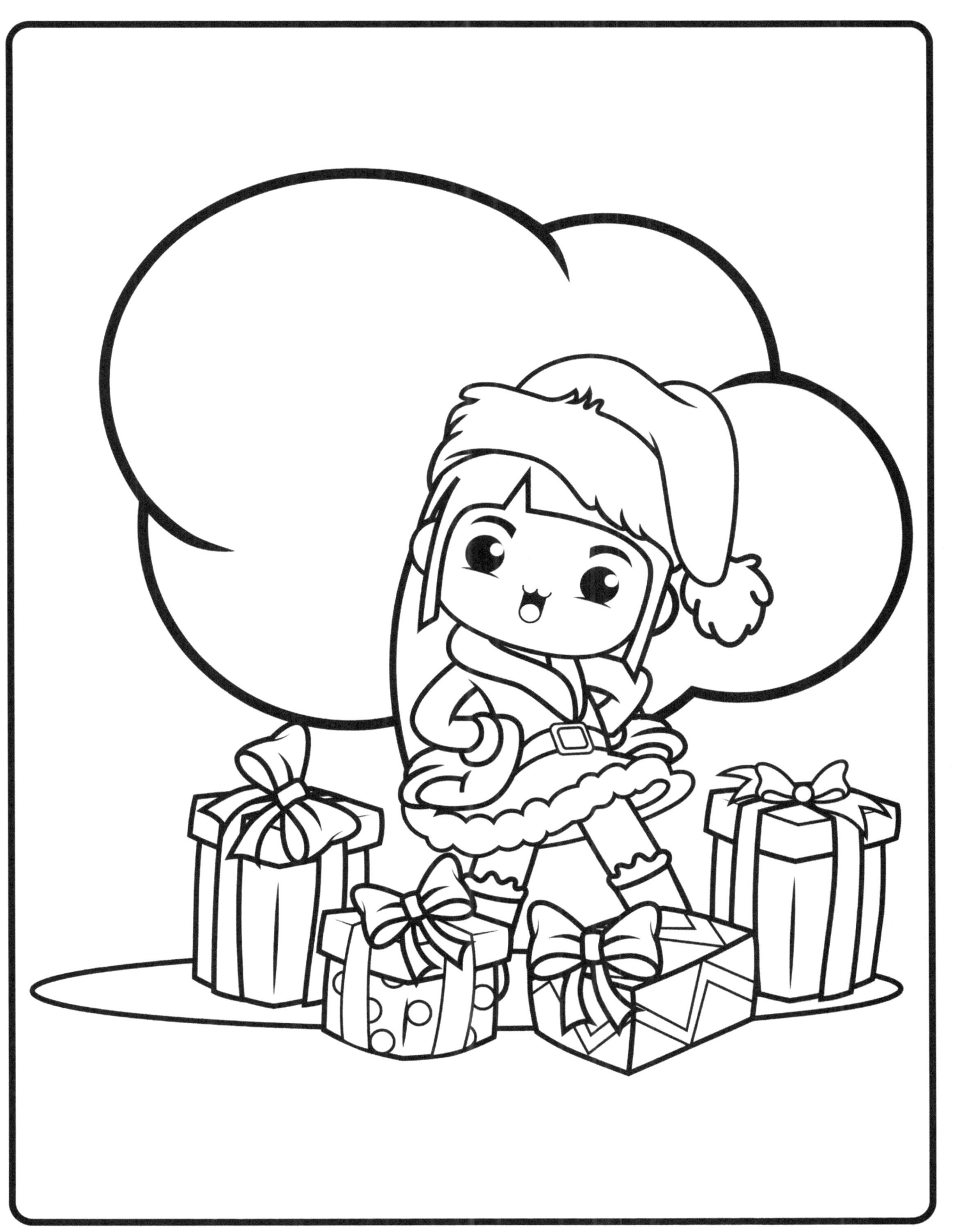

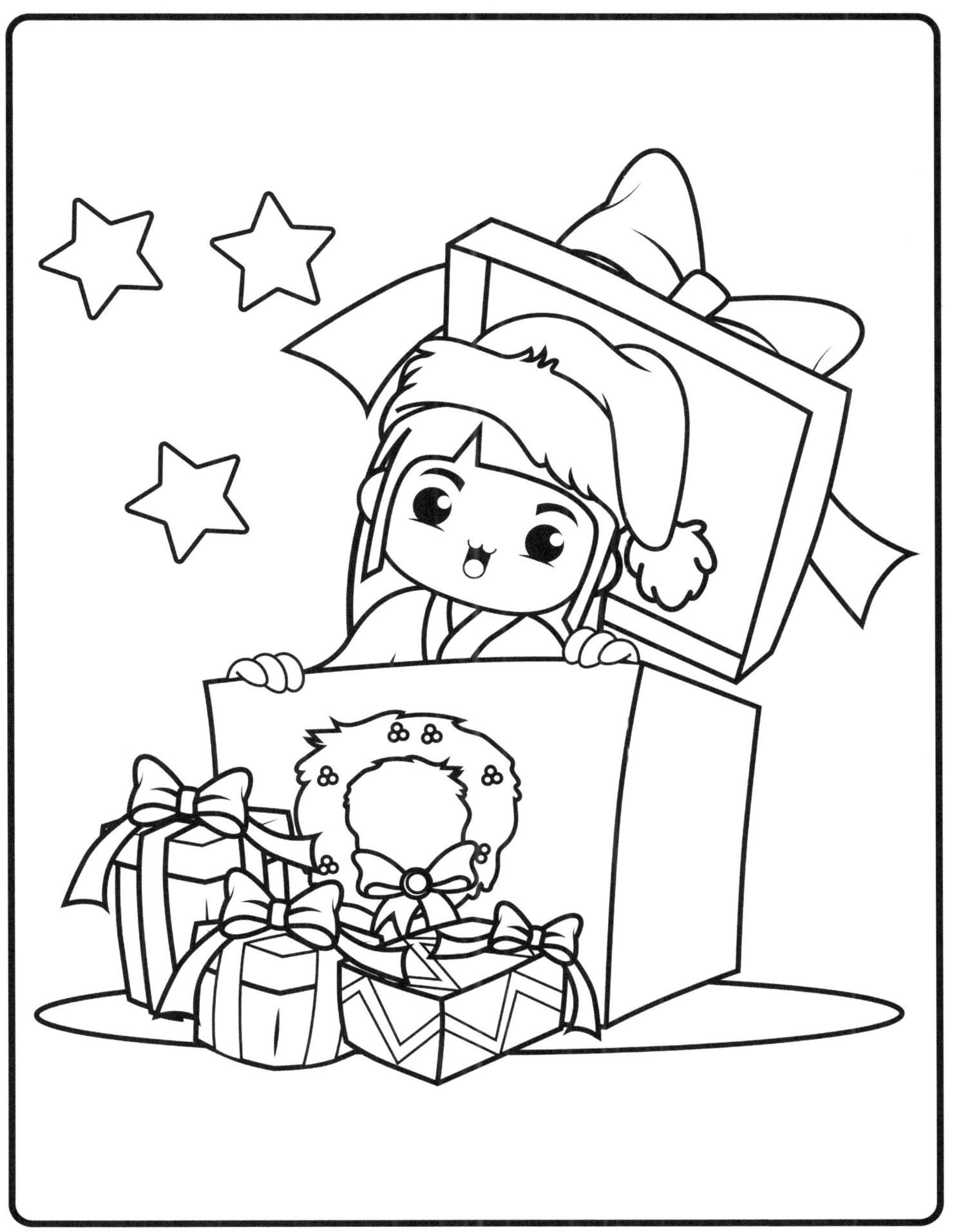

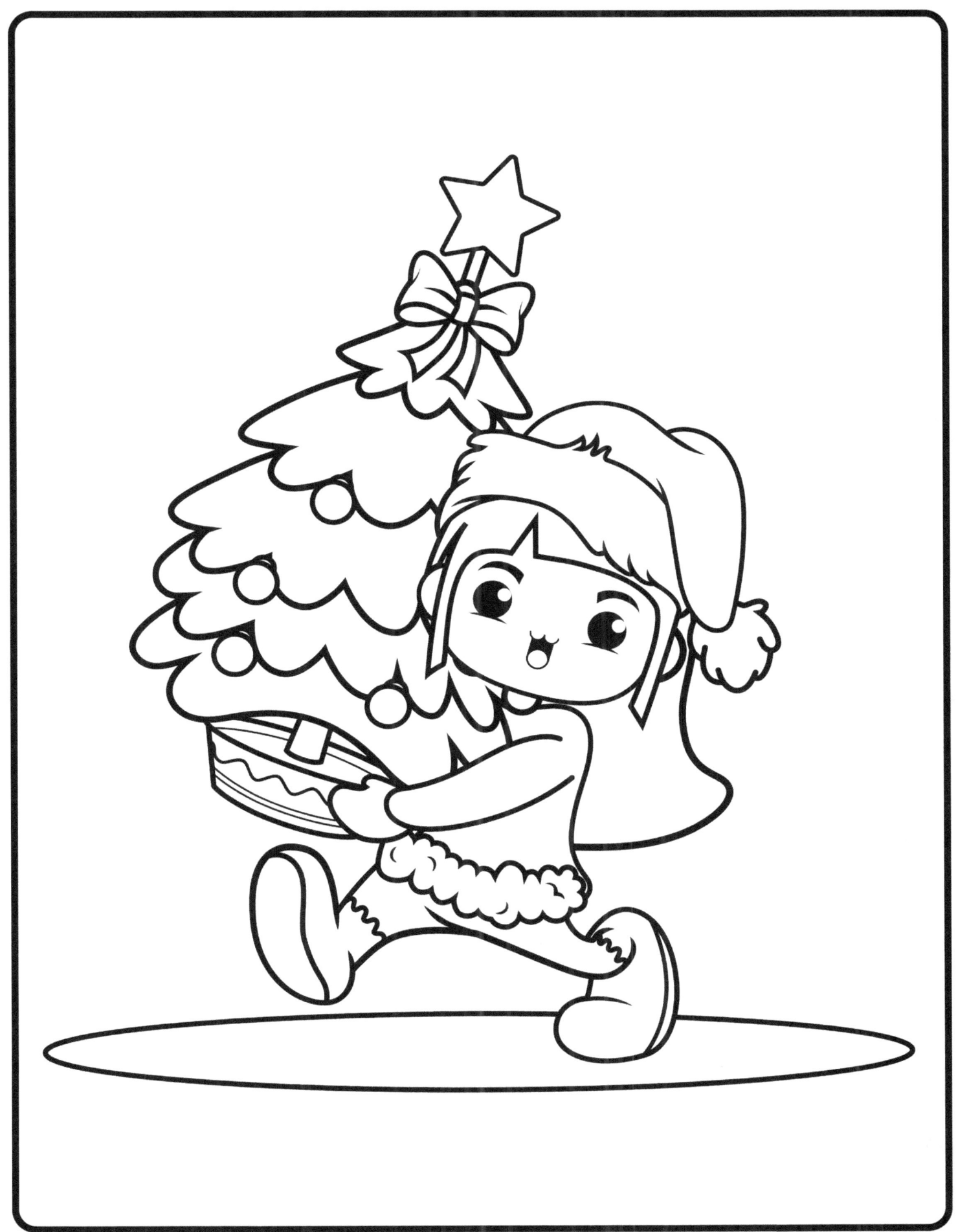

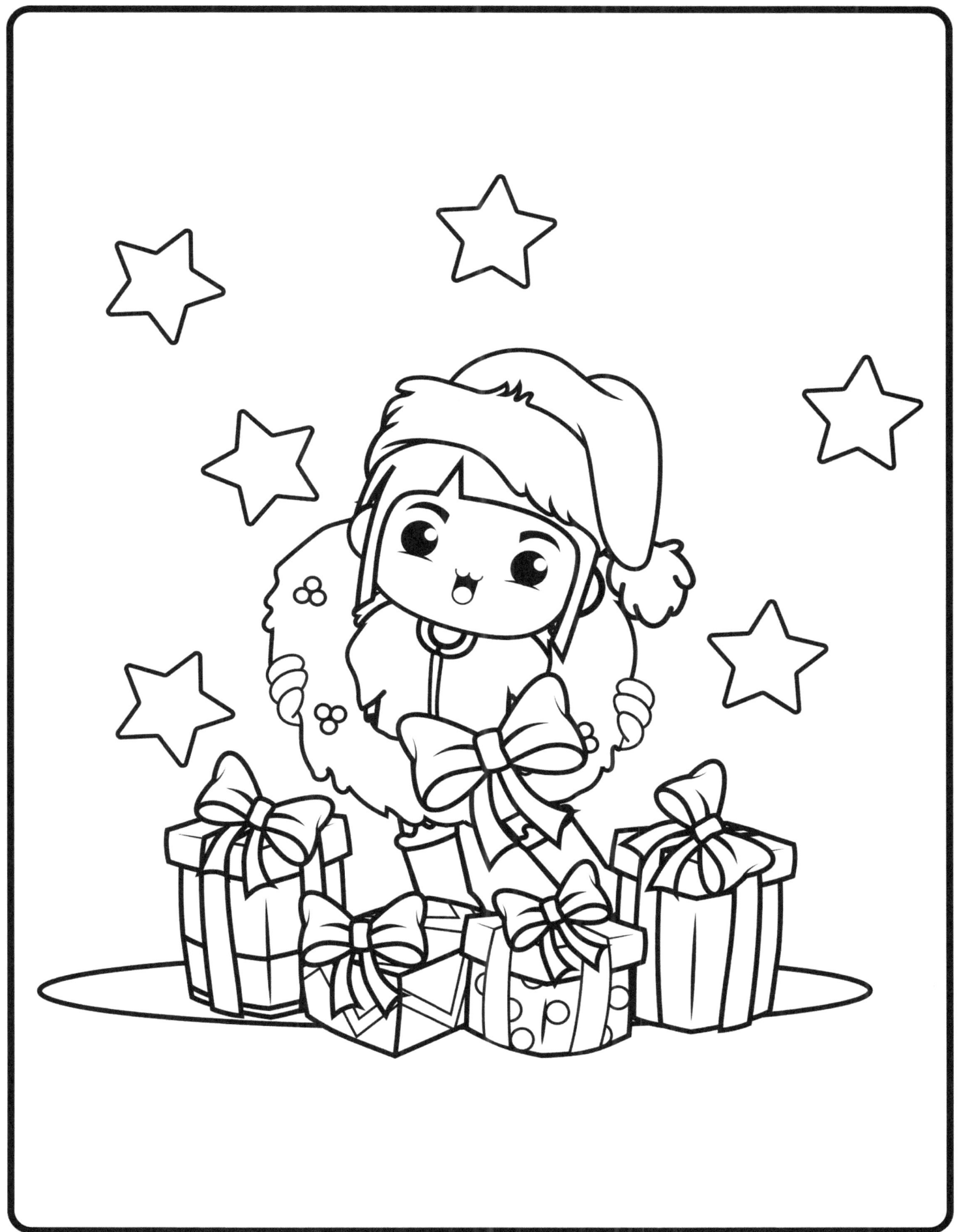

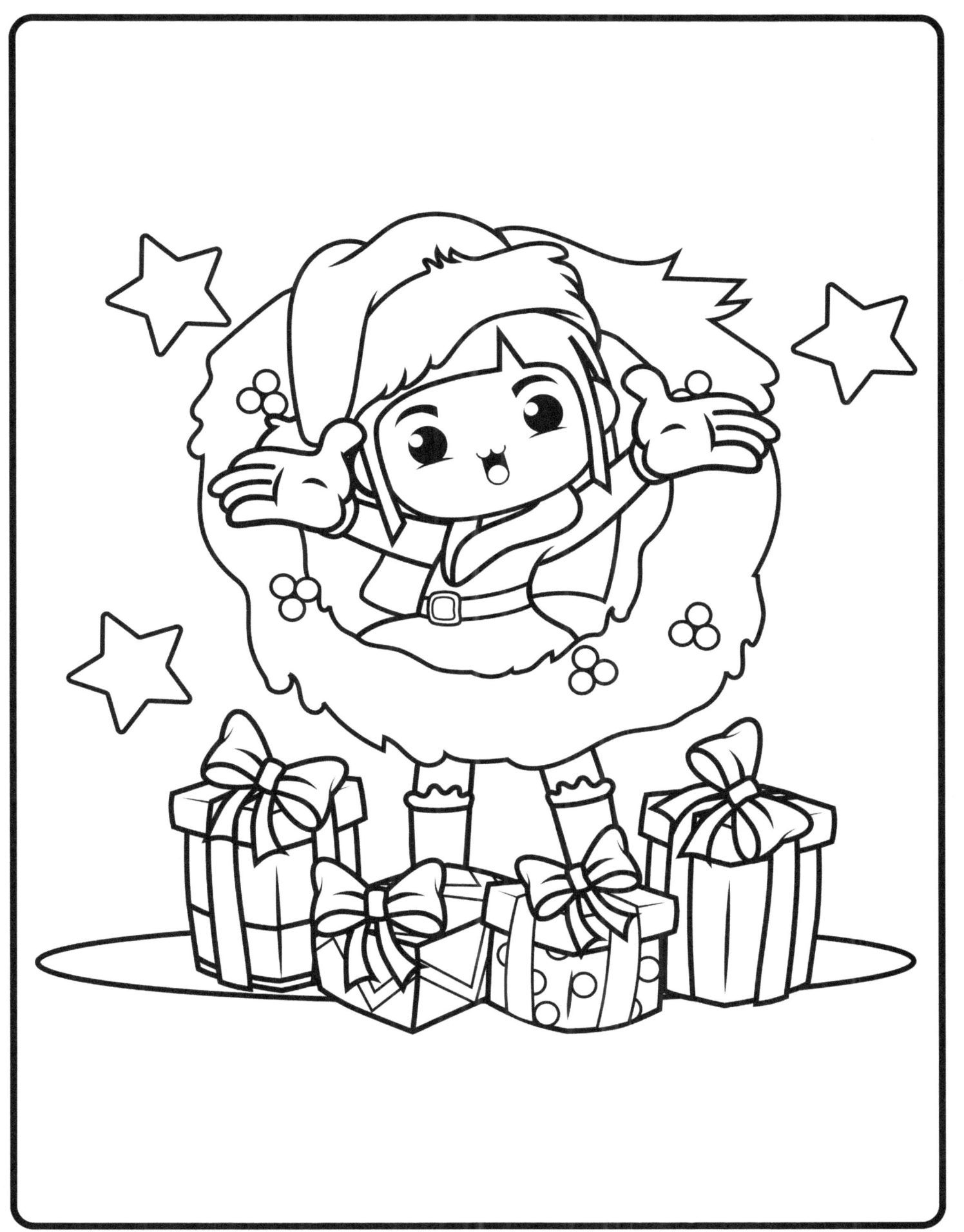

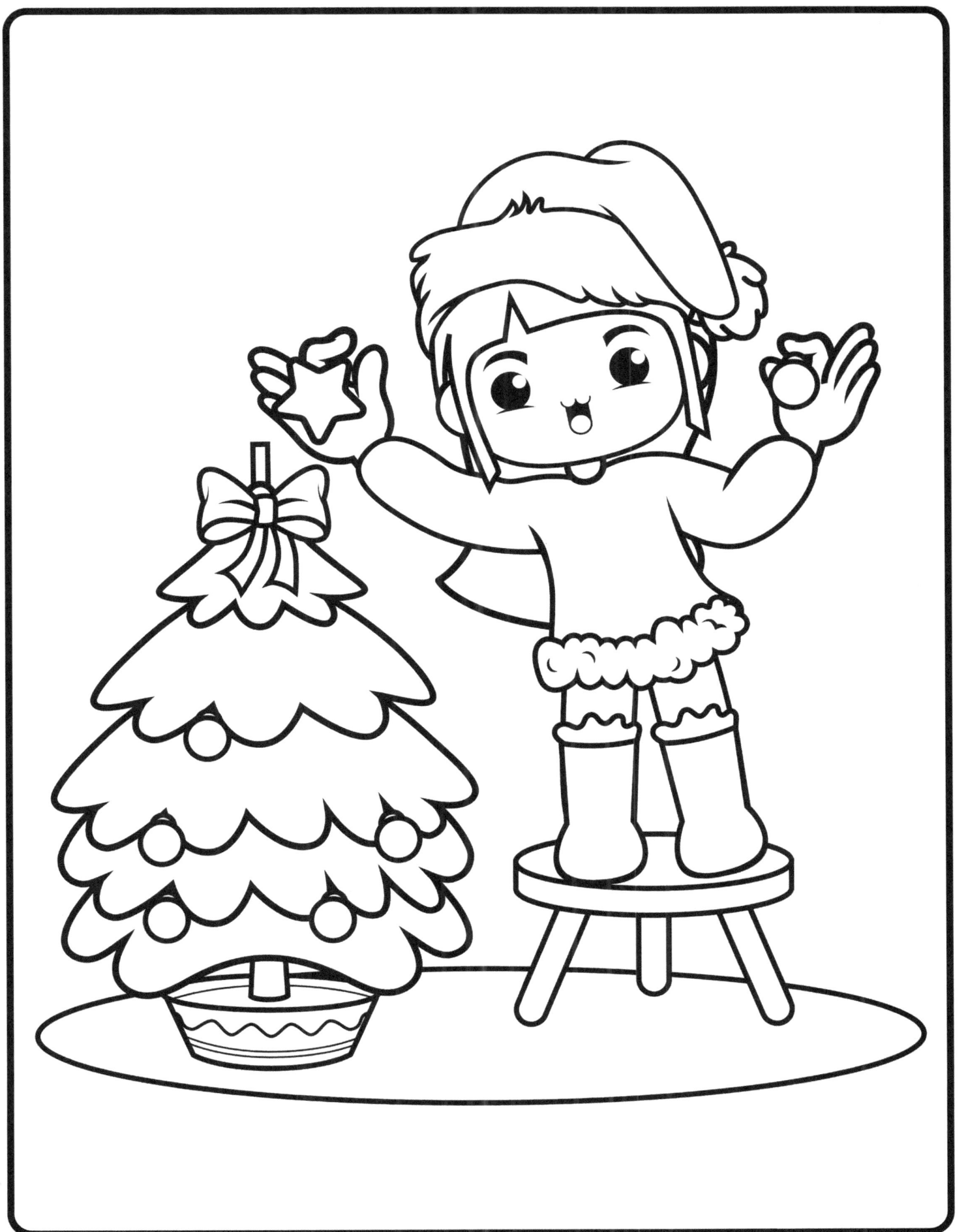

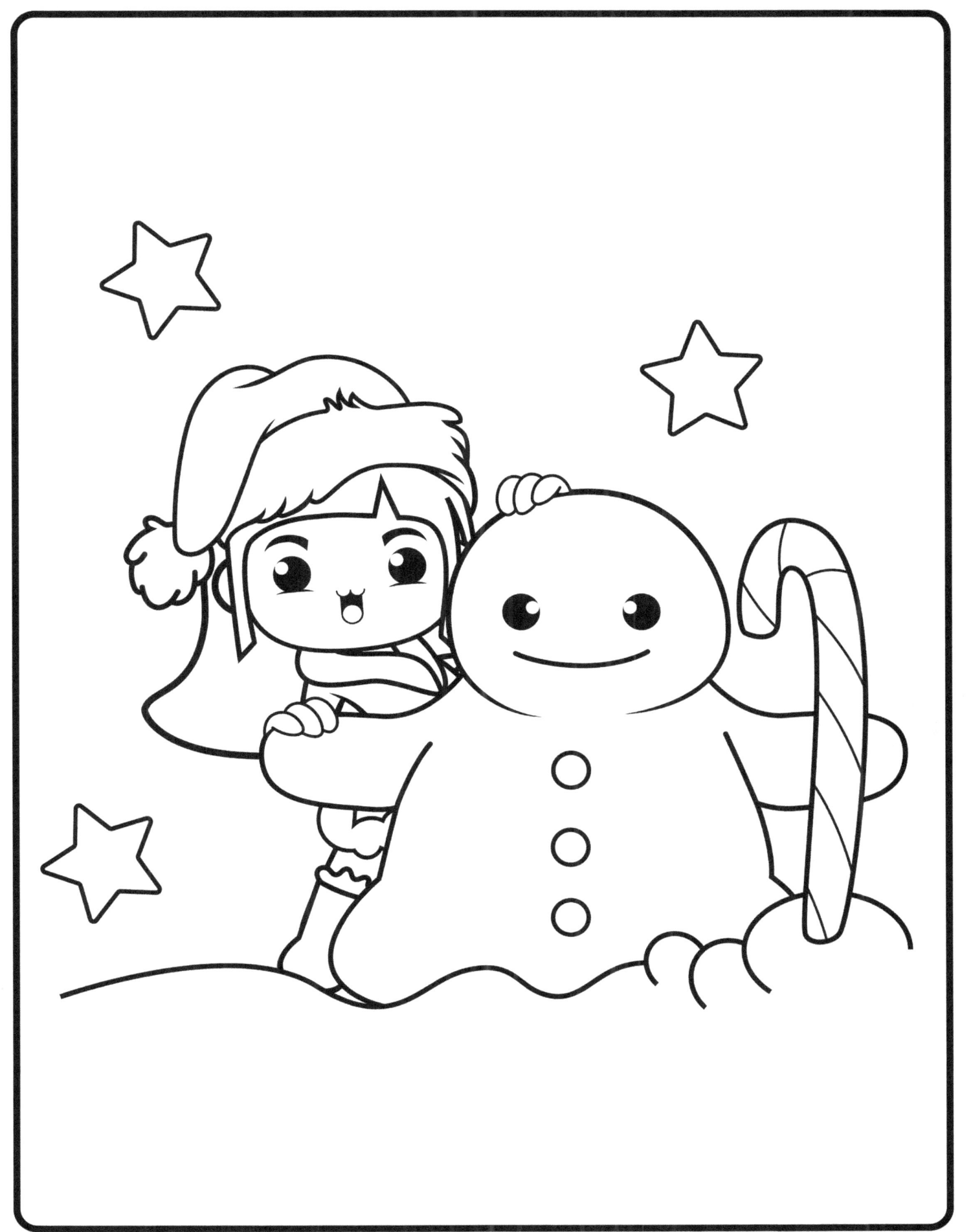

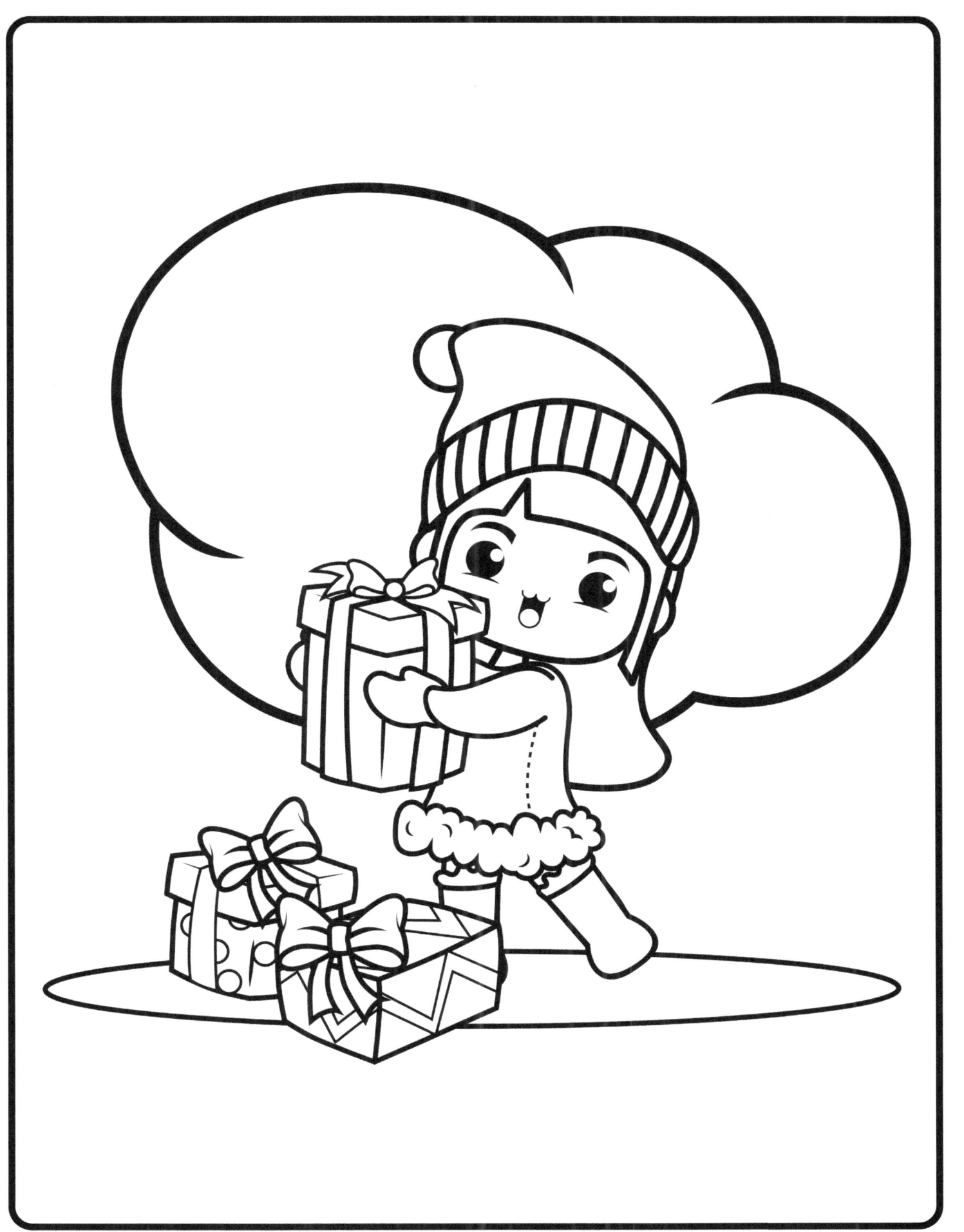

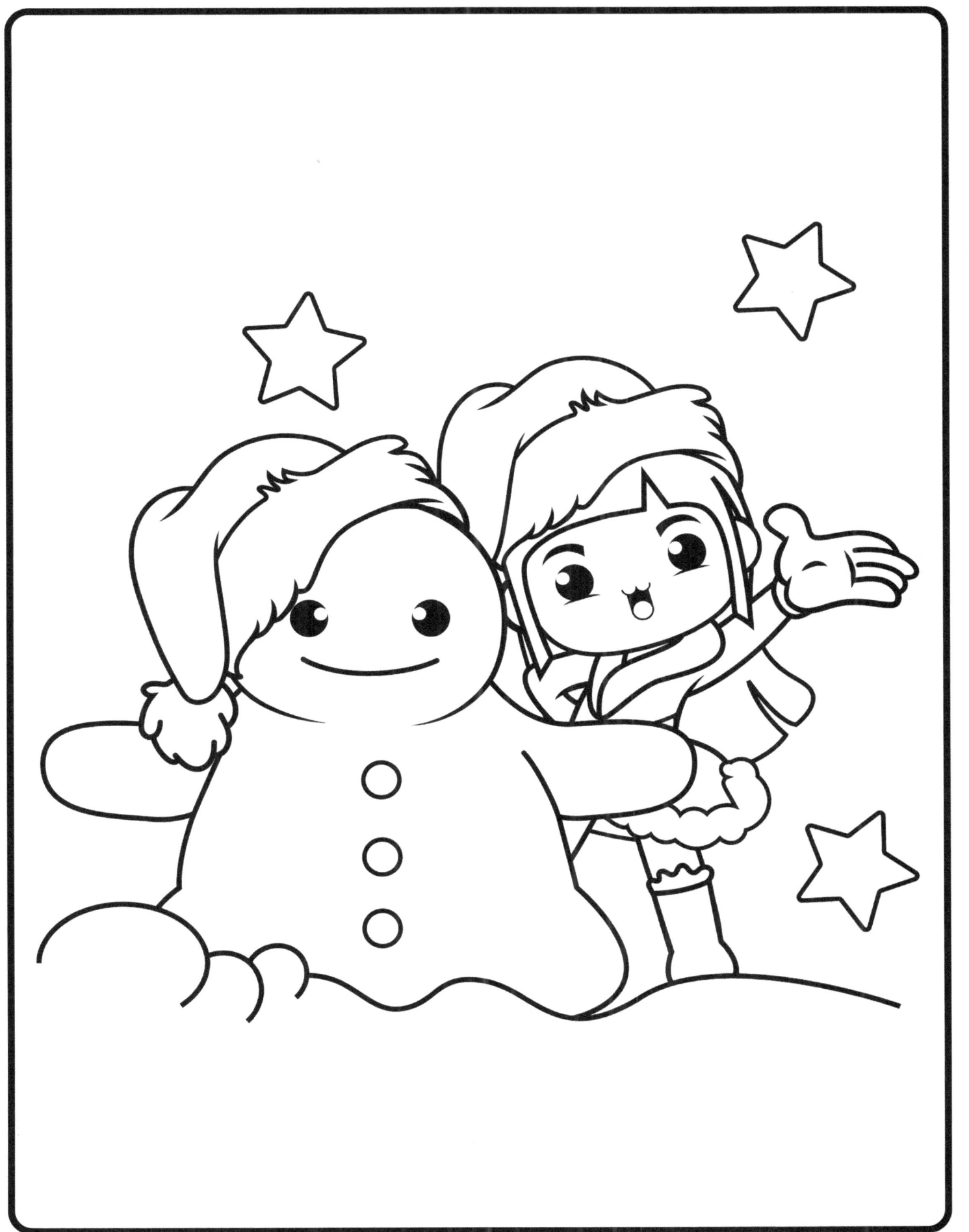

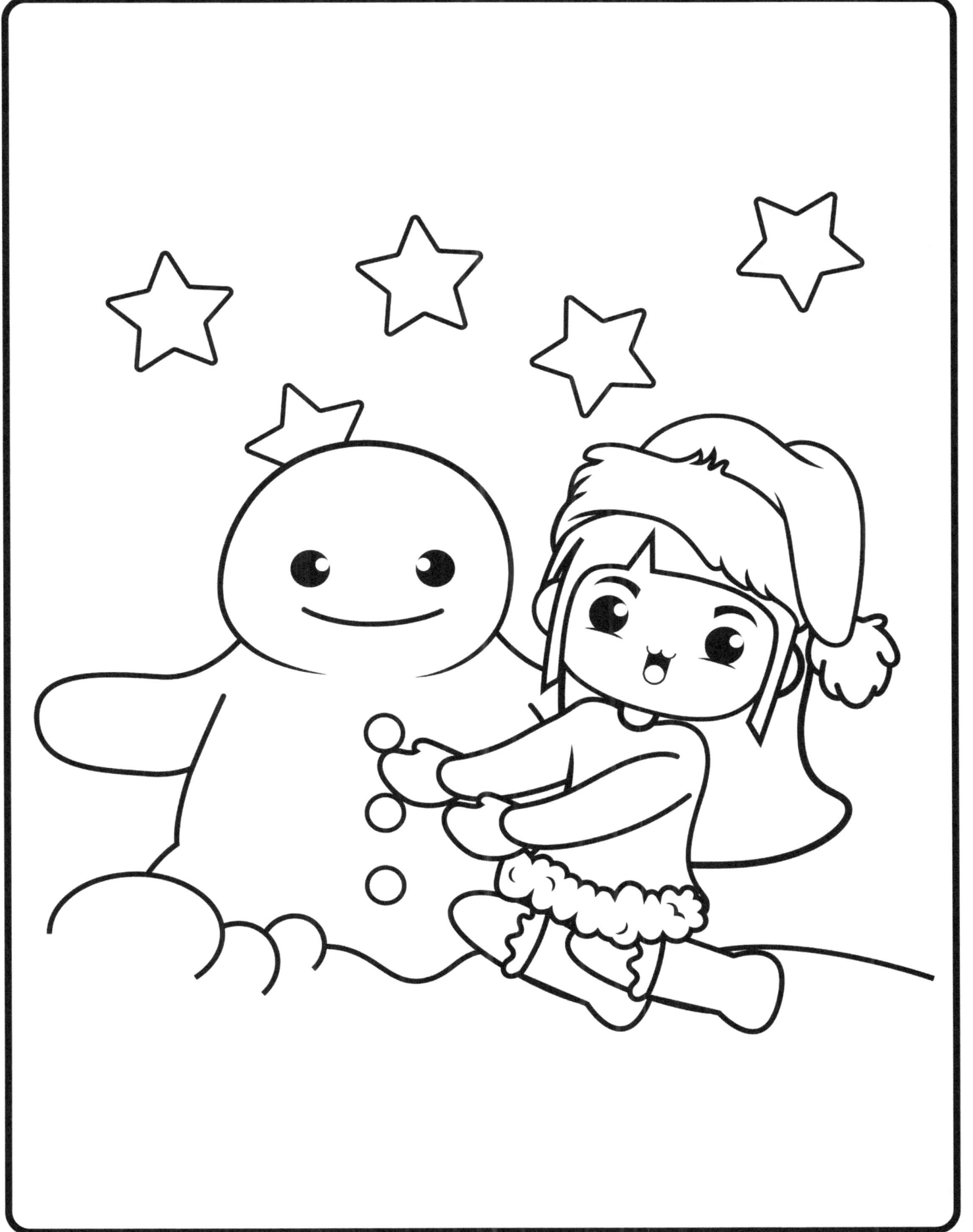

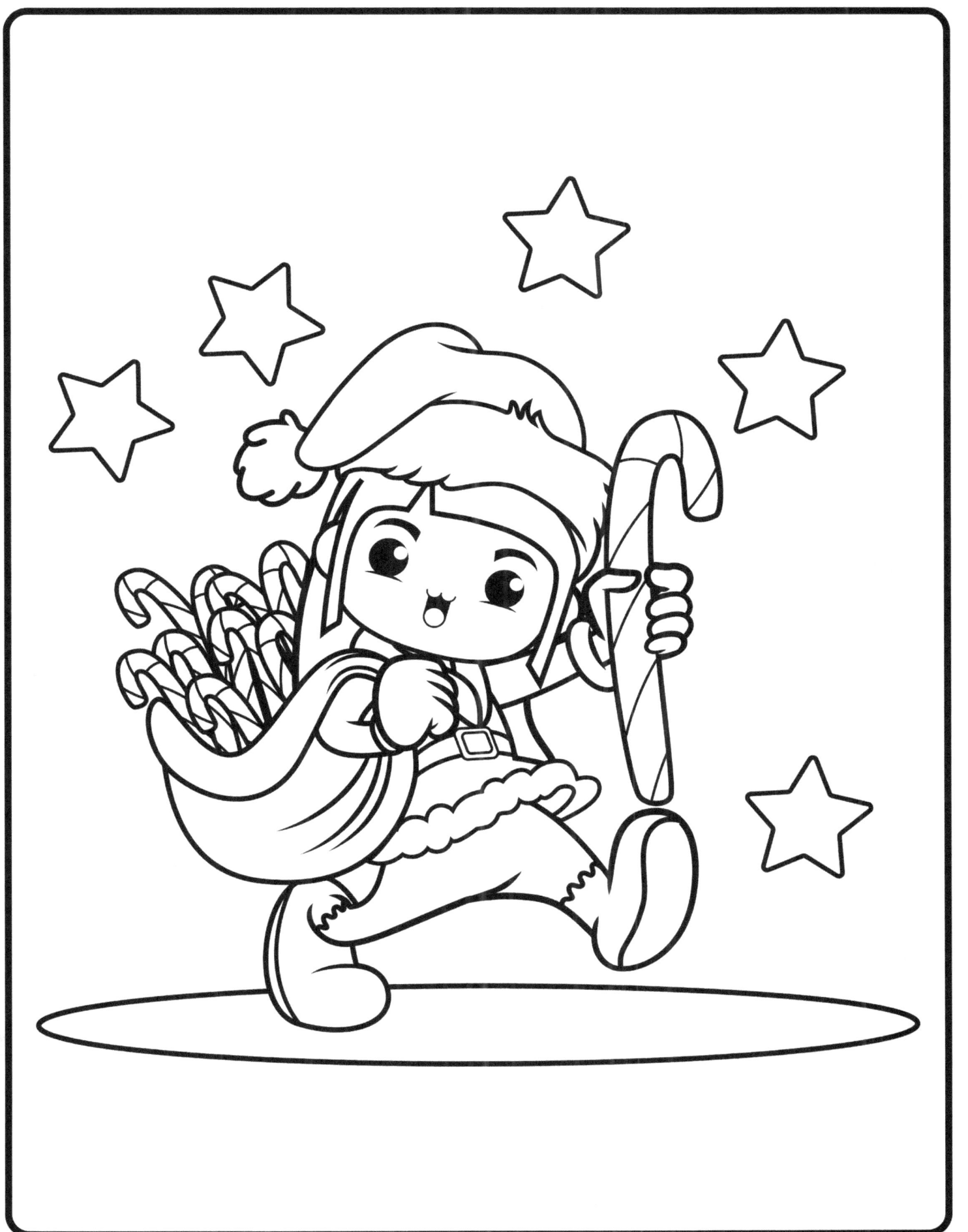

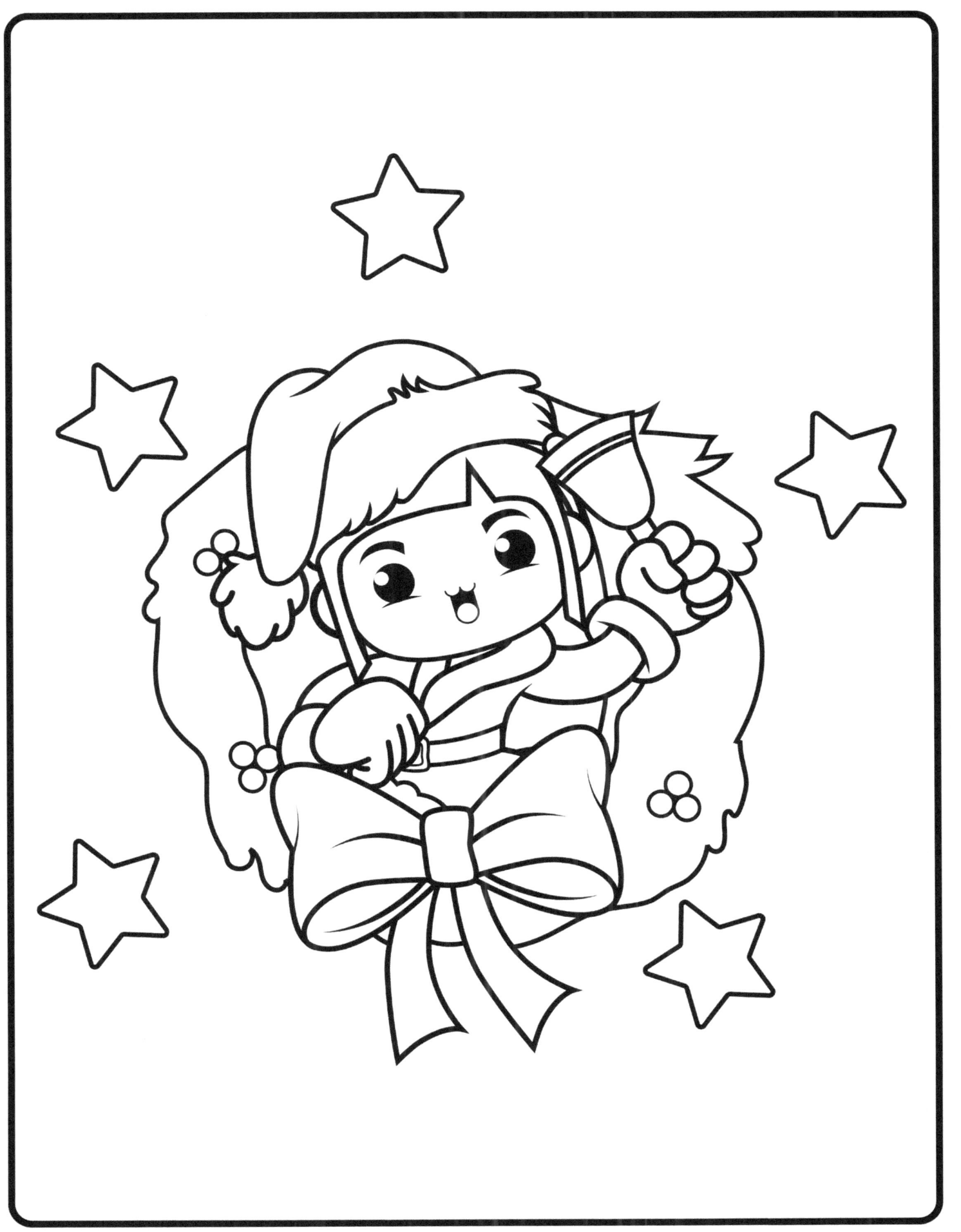

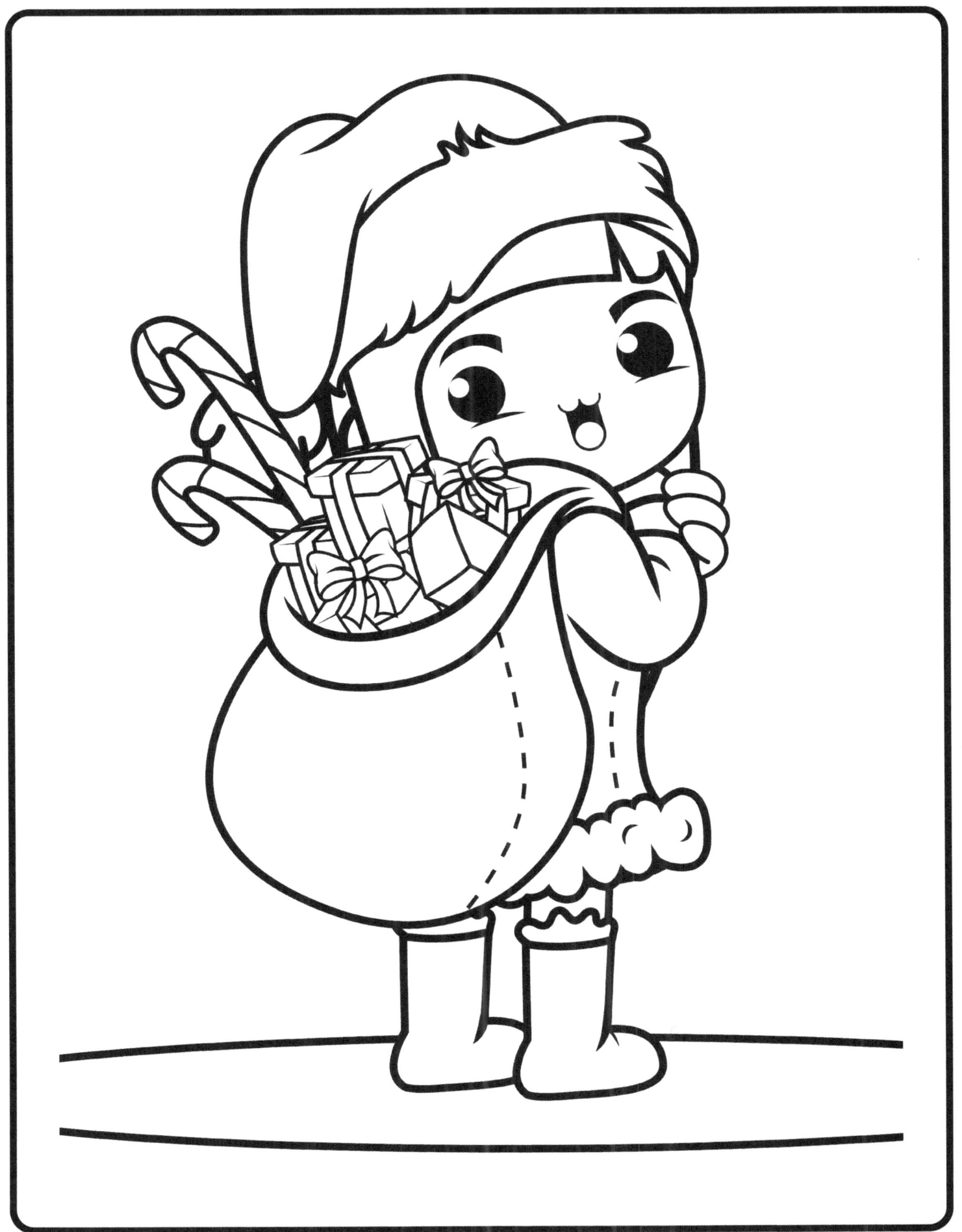

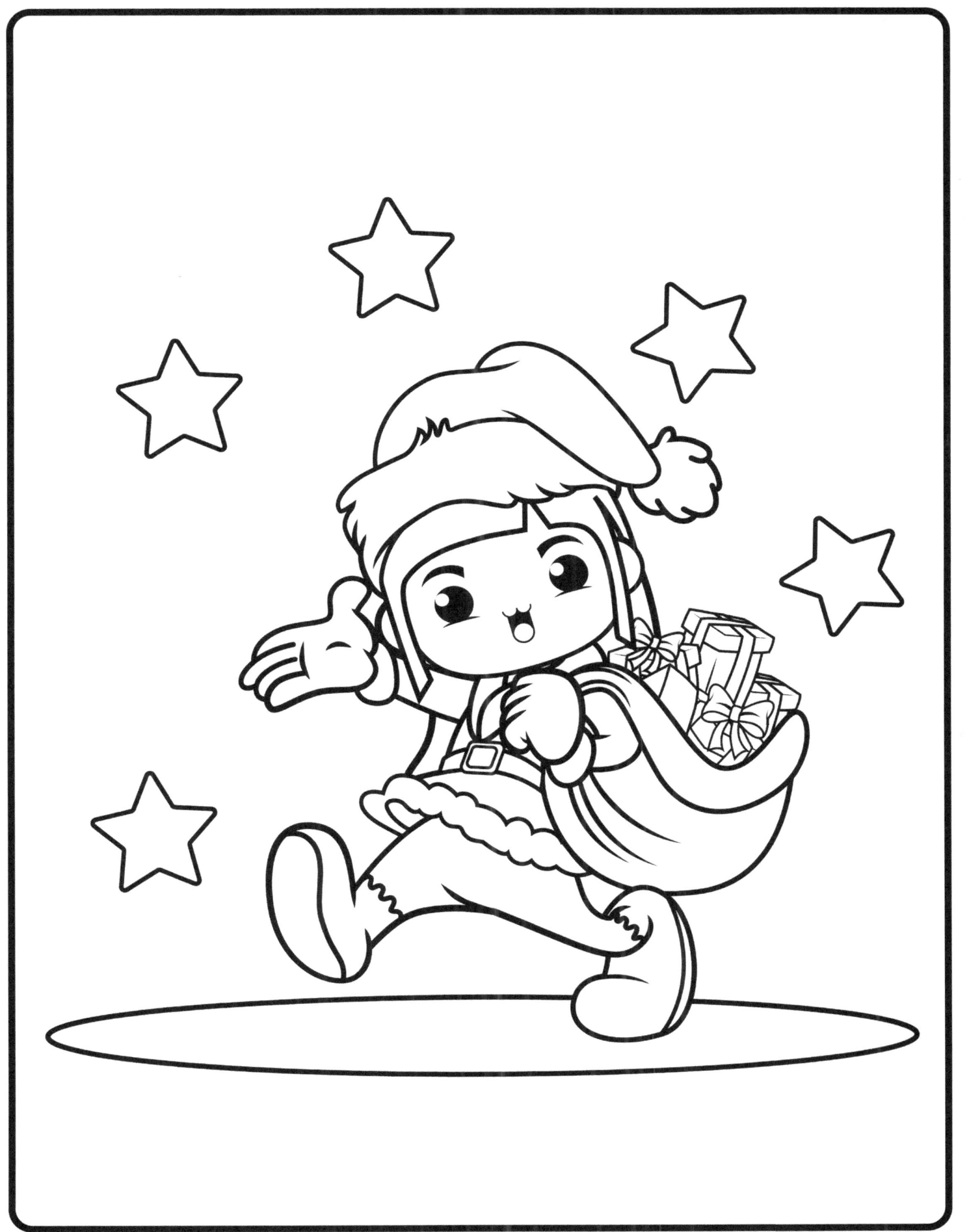

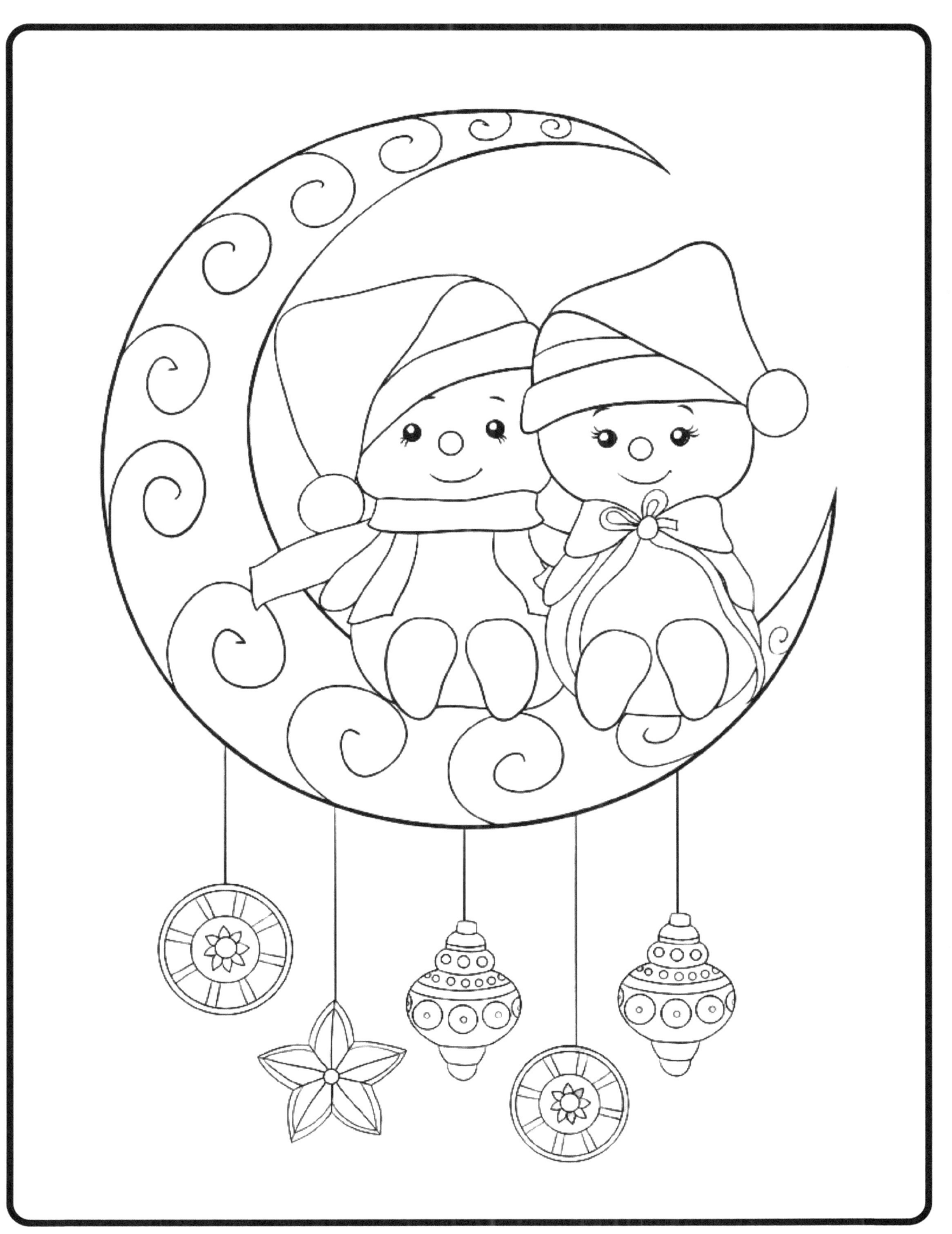

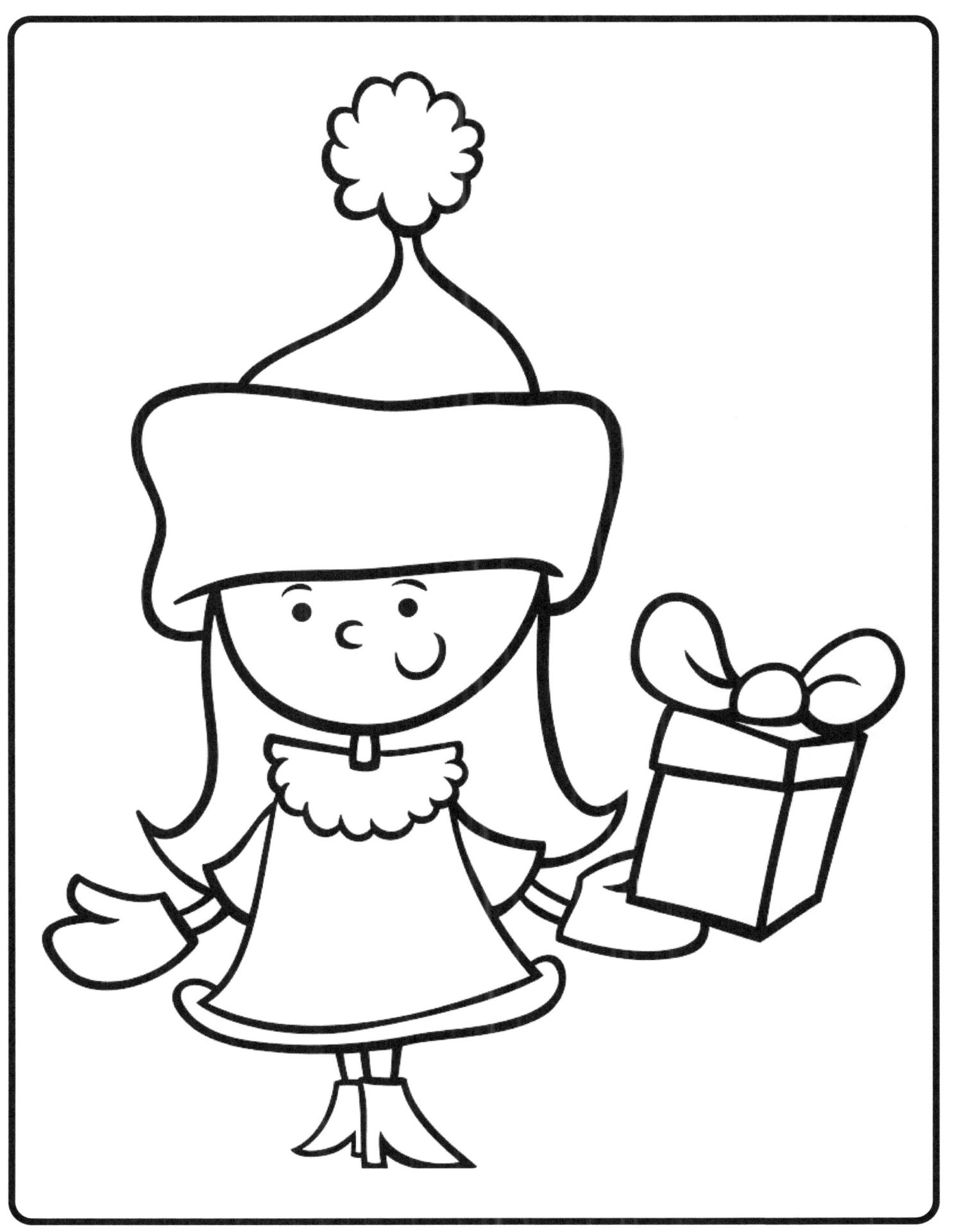

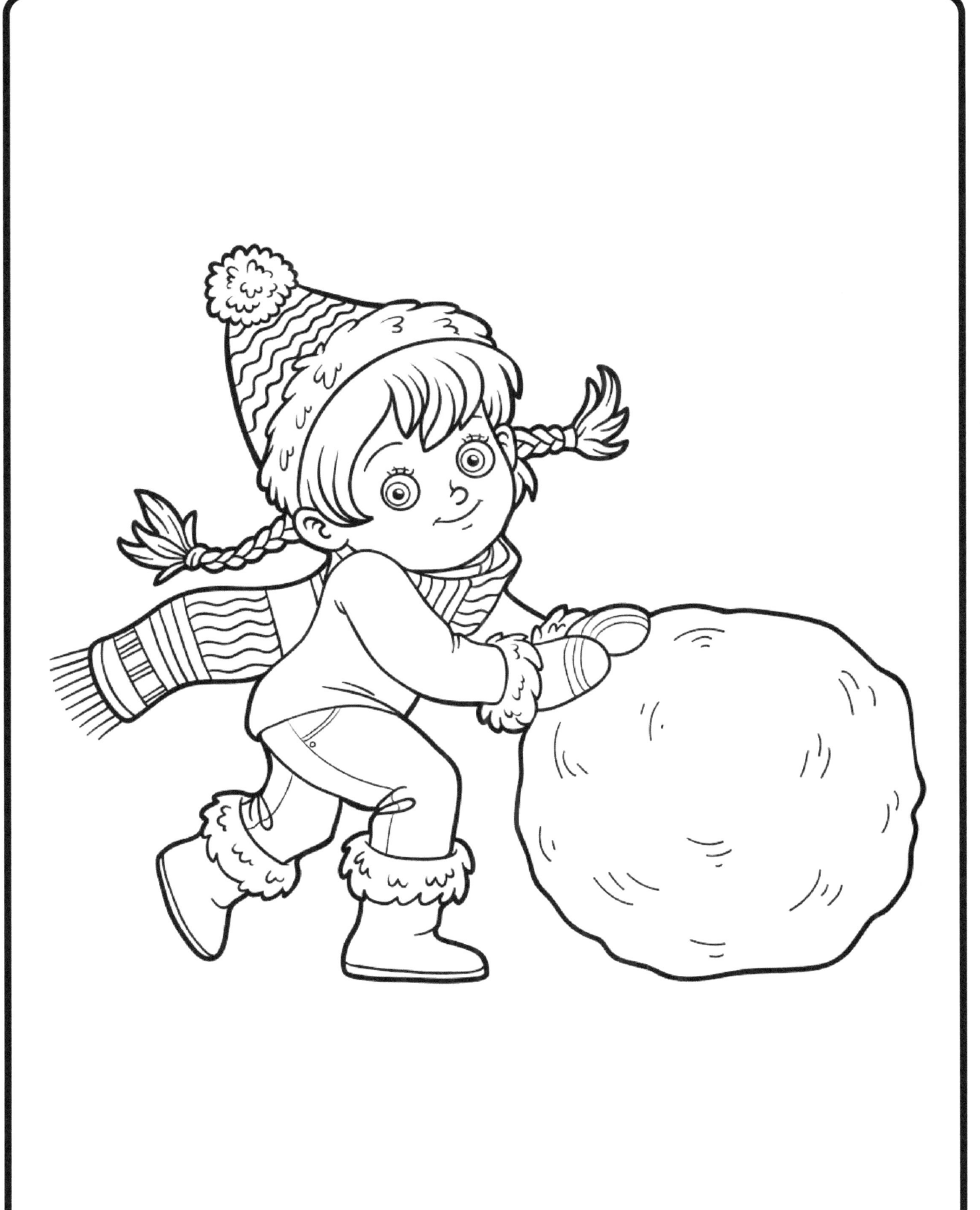

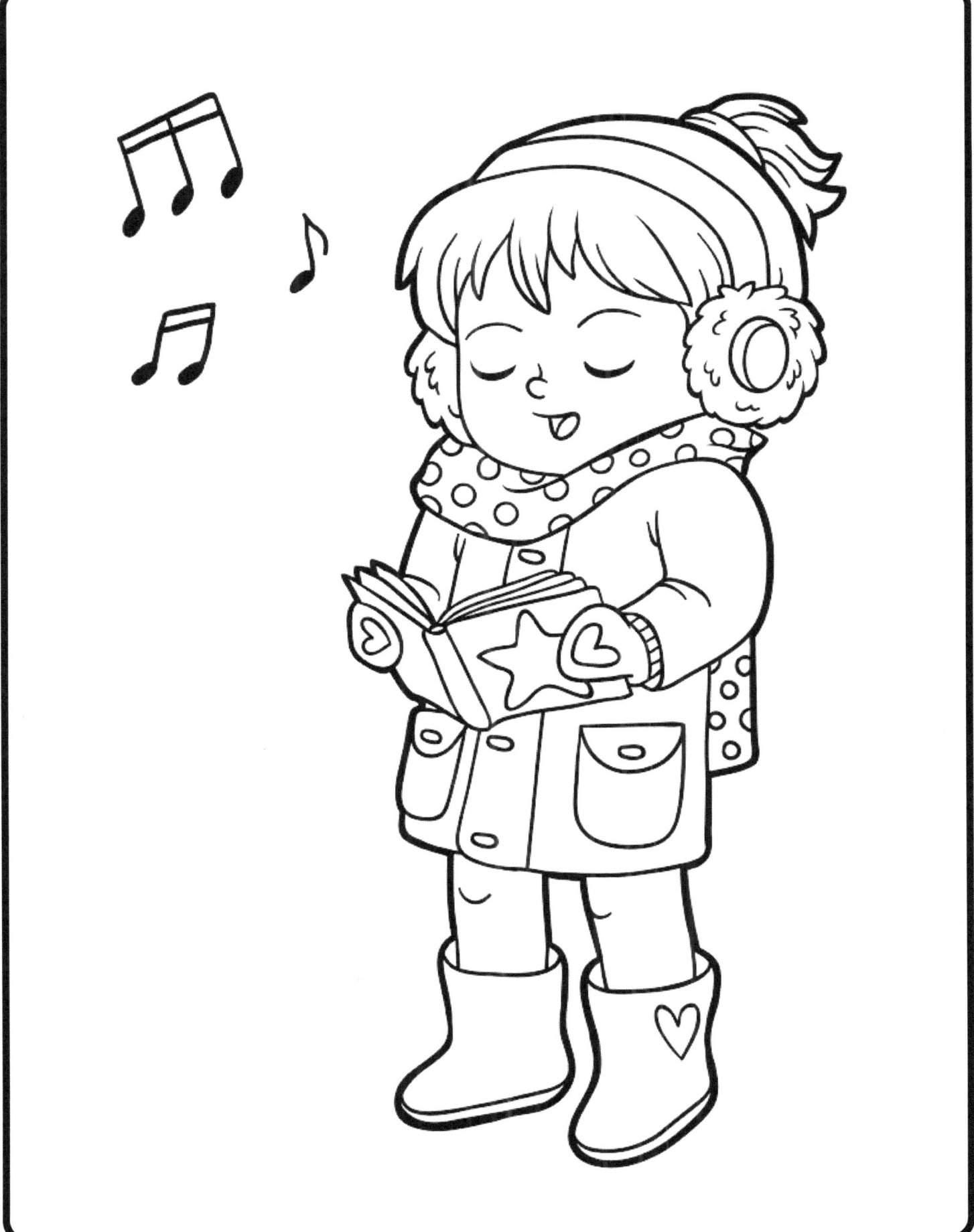

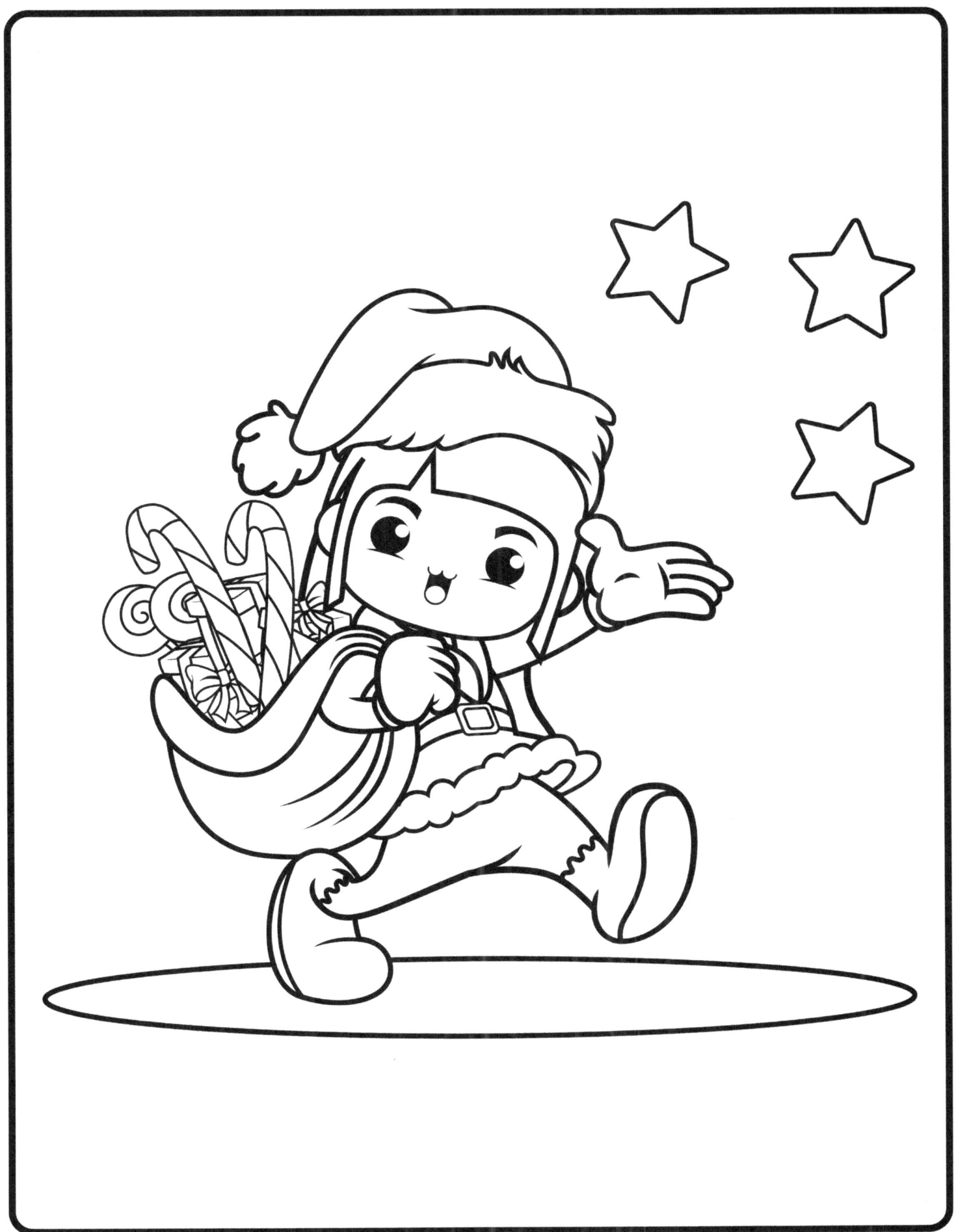

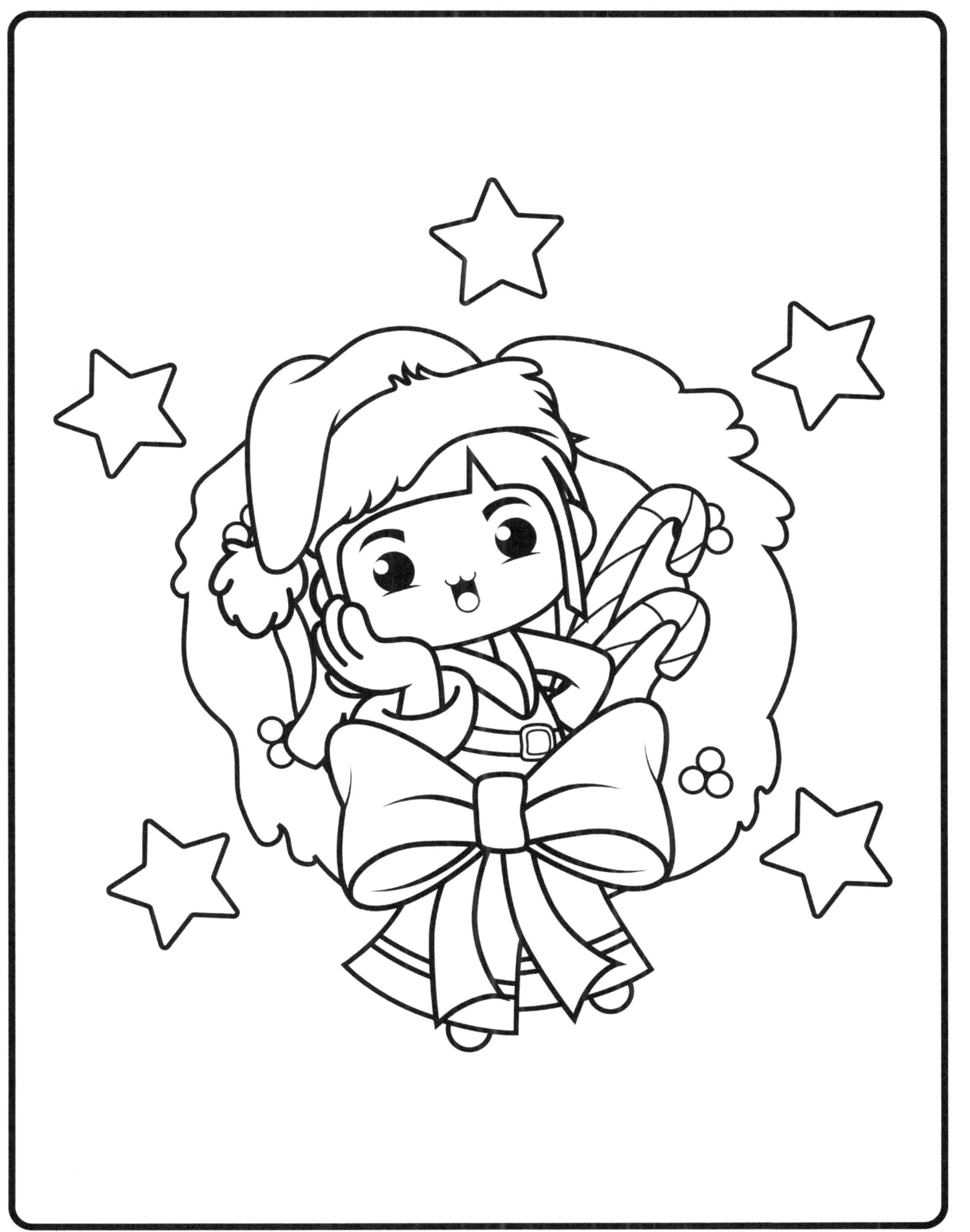

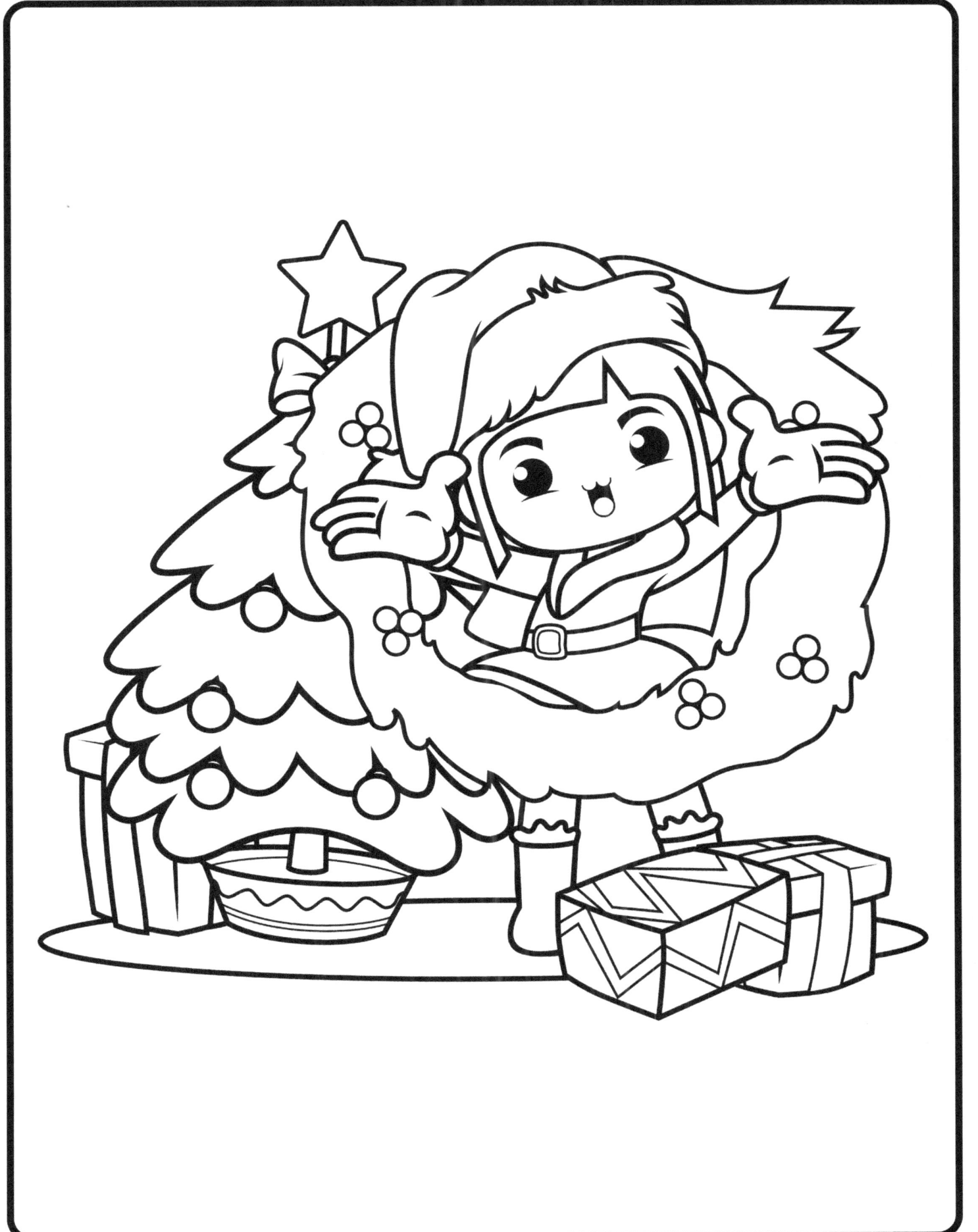

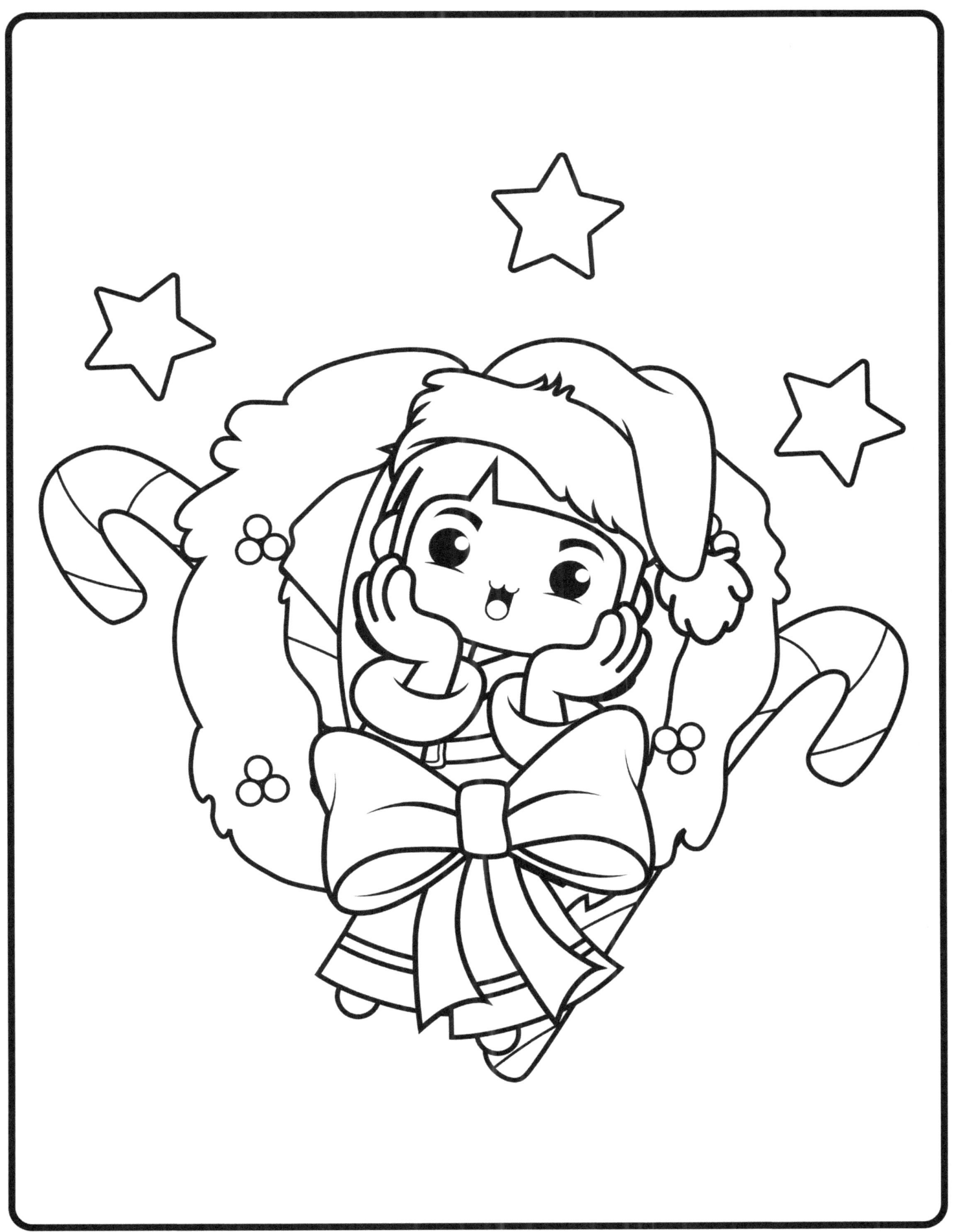

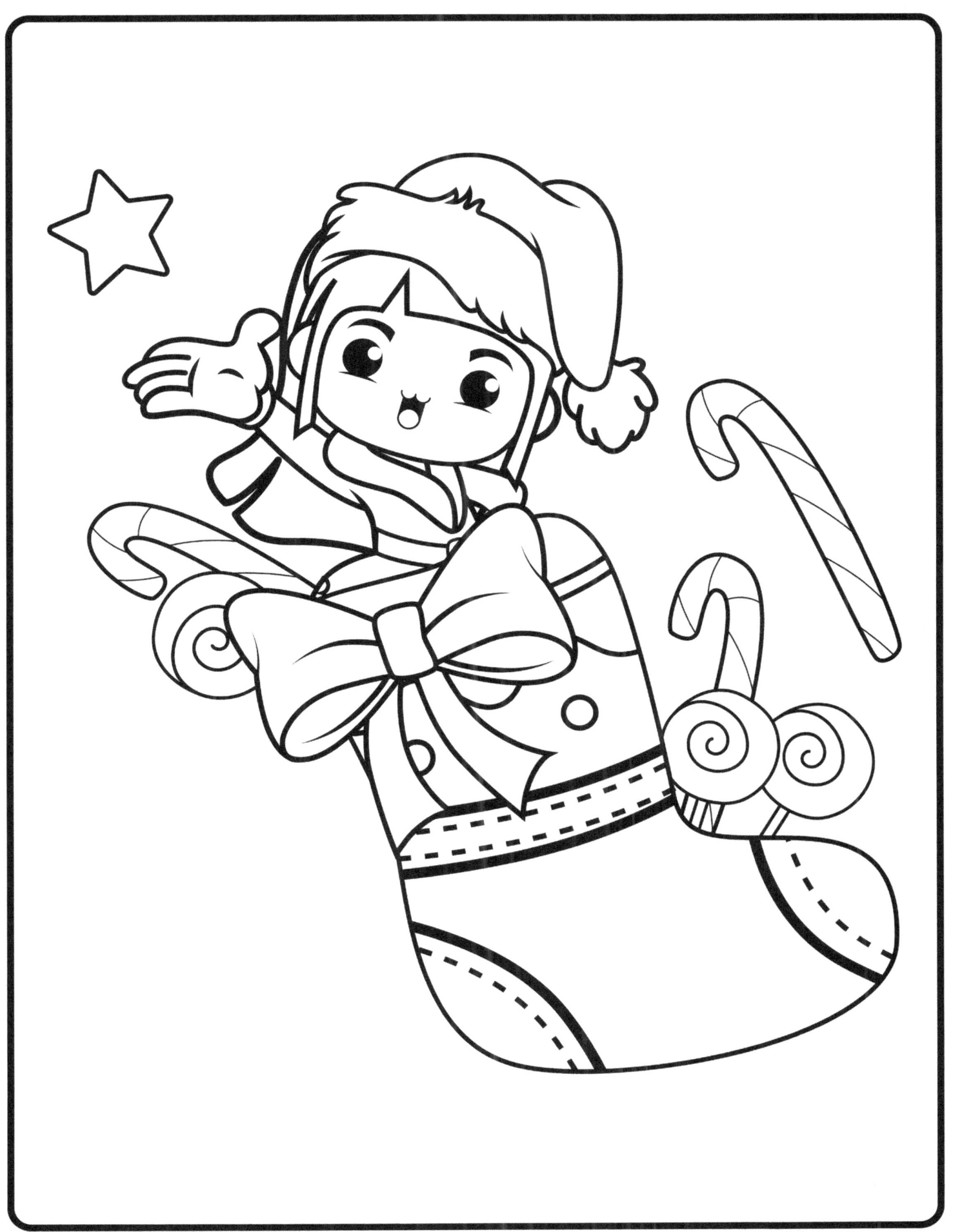

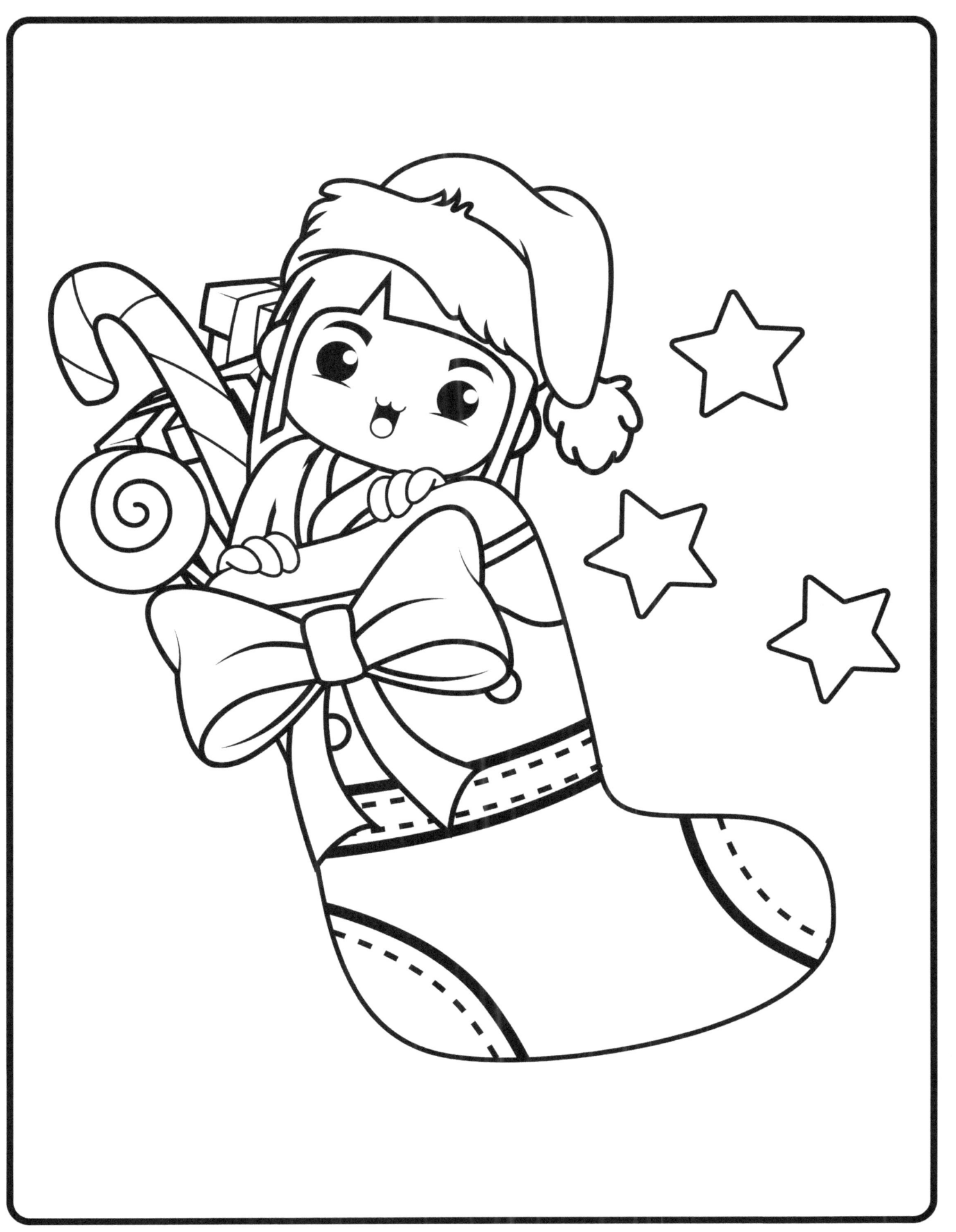

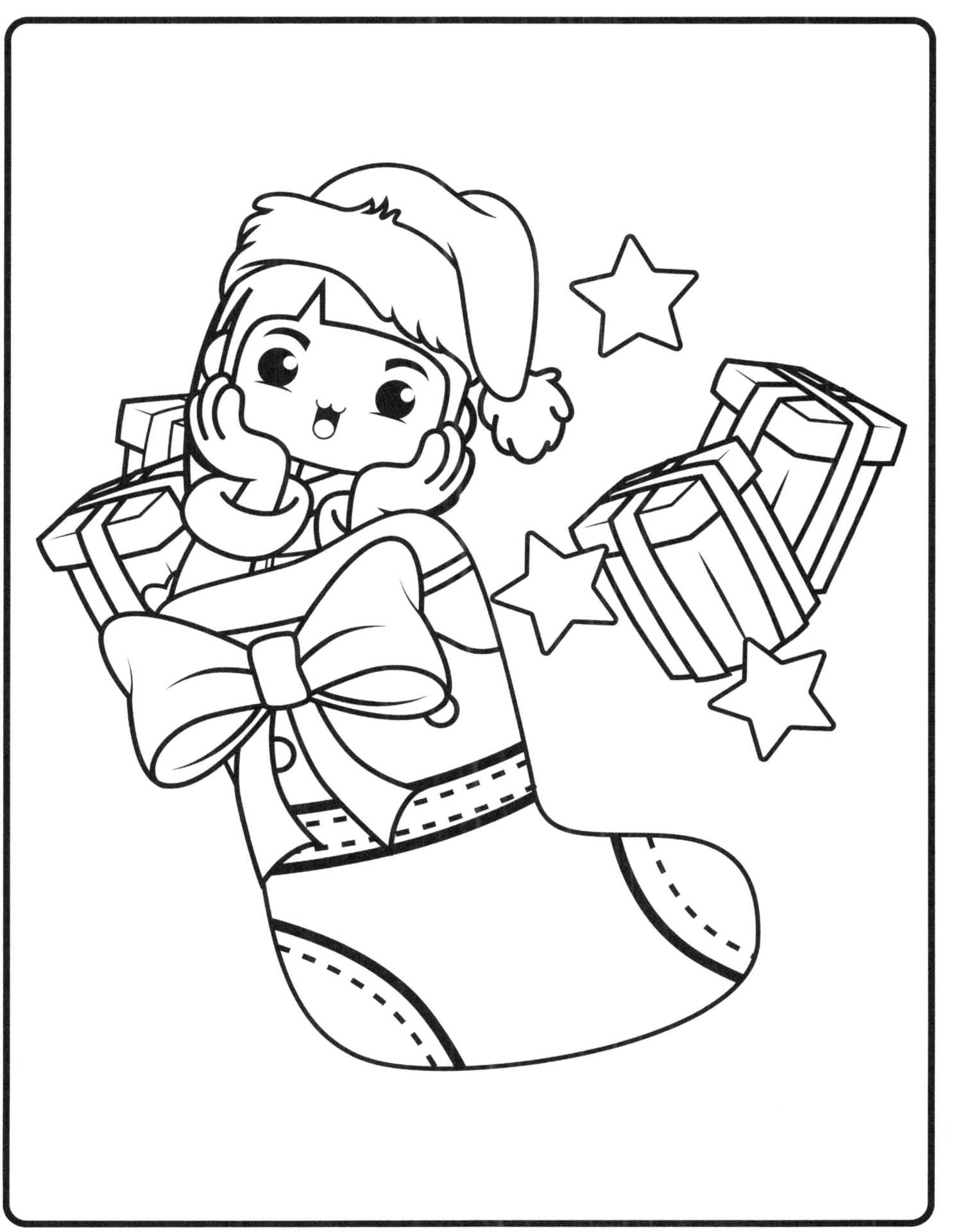

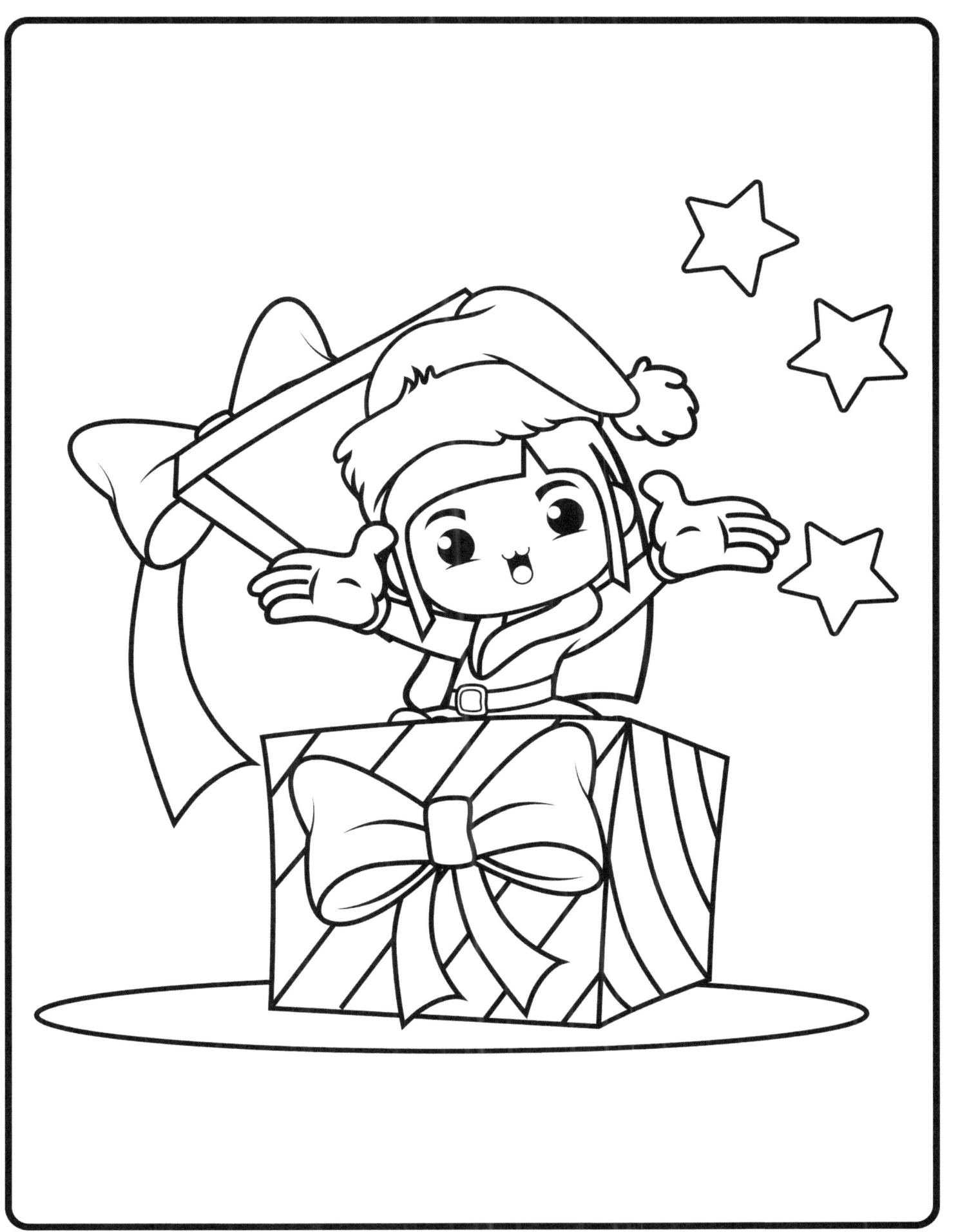

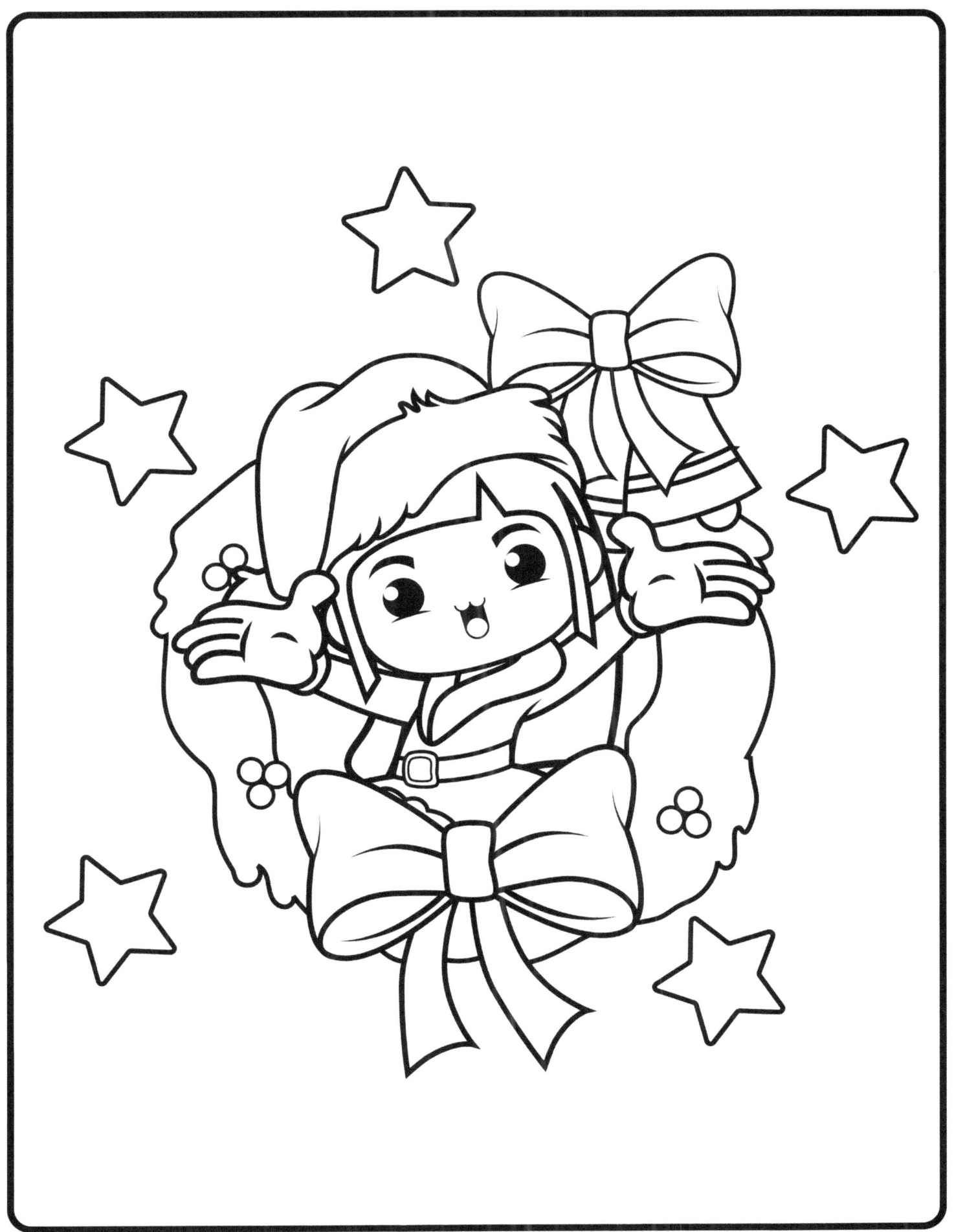

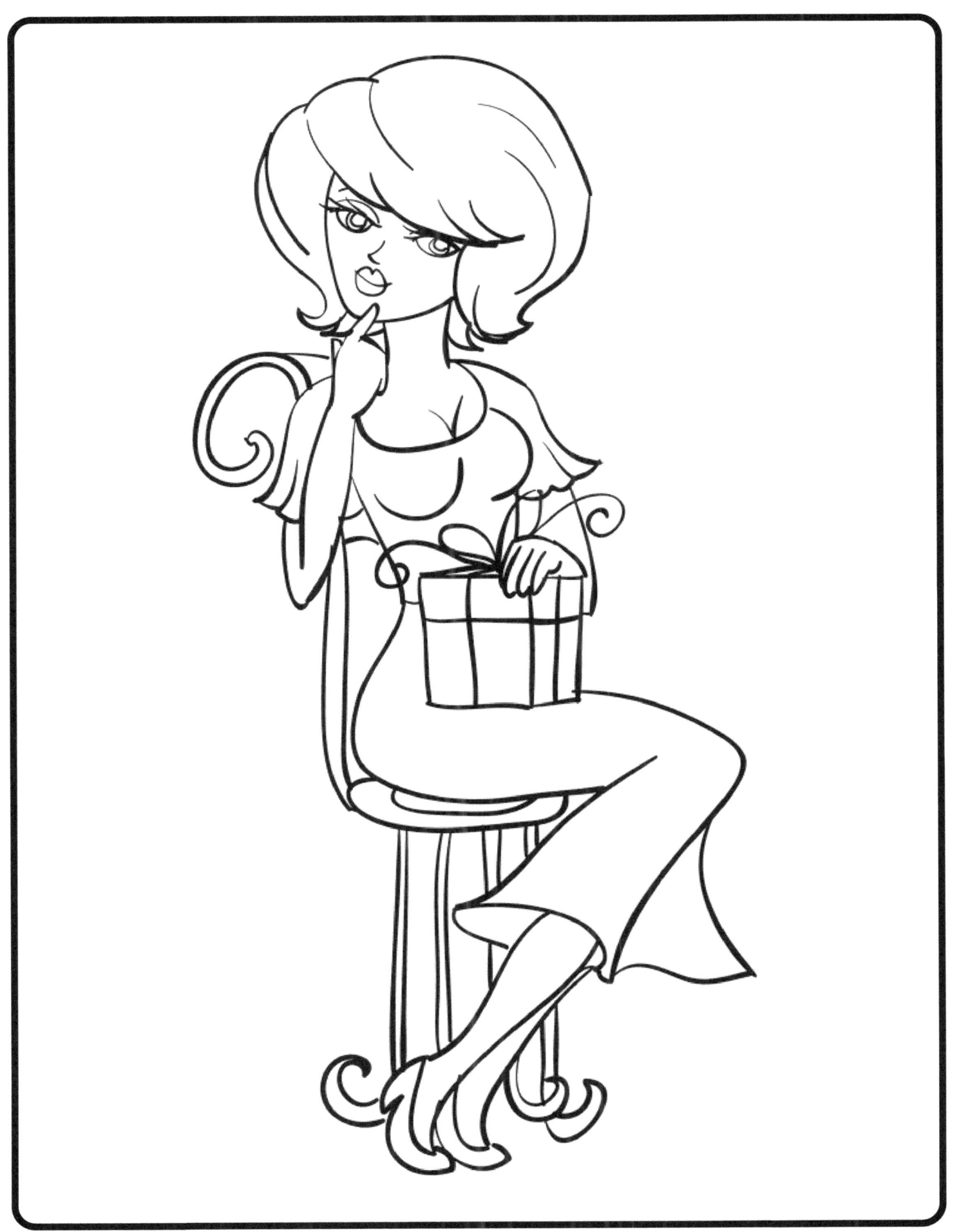

www.ingramcontent.com/pod-product-compliance
Lightning Source LLC
Chambersburg PA
CBHW080619220526
45466CB00010B/3396